September 11

a case for

The Higher Purpose

LAUREN TRATAR

Our Mission

To inspire and empower others to live life as a
magical experience. By simplifying ageless wisdom
into practical tools and techniques,
we intend to improve the quality of life,
alleviate unnecessary pain,
and simultaneously recreate our world.

© 2002

by Lauren J. Tratar

First Edition 2002

ISBN 0-9704030-9-7

WWW.SECRETTOLIFE.NET

1-888-762-7808

Published by:

An Alliance of Angels Publishing Company

P.O. Box 3368 Lisle, Illinois 60532

Printed in Canada

...and the Great Phoenix was seen rising up from the smouldering ashes of the earth. It's iridescent purple feathers catching the sunlight and reflecting the blinding beacons out onto the land — beacons that were the sign of the world's regeneration, its new age of awareness and eternal peace.

— MARY SUMMER RAIN
Phoenix Rising: No Eyes' Vision of the Changes to Come

This book is dedicated
to those
who
" crossed over "
on September 11, 2001

From the Author

"Grasshopper, look beyond the game, as you look beneath the surface of the pool to see its depths."
— MASTER PO
from the TV show "Kung Fu"

A higher purpose to the unconscionable terrorist attacks of September 11? Is that just plain malarkey, the mind searching for answers to the incomprehensible? Were these horrific events, events that changed life as we knew it, simply a random act of violence, or could there be a deeper meaning underlying them? As one woman put it, "If September 11 did *not* have a higher purpose, what's the point?"

Although nothing we do or say will bring back those who lost their lives on that fateful day, perhaps our pain would be eased if we found that a higher purpose was underlying these tragedies; a purpose that transcended blame and victimhood; ideally, a purpose that ushered in something of importance for humankind. But simply pondering that notion opens a big can of worms, does it not? For if there is a higher purpose to what occurred on September 11, that implies there must be a higher purpose for everything that occurs, right?

Allow me to present a case for the Higher Purpose of September 11, which at the same time, will shed light on the higher purpose for everything that occurs in life. My 'evidence' is gleaned from a number of diverse sources, each contributing a piece to the 'puzzle of life' that must now be connected if we are to ever understand why and how tragic events occur.

My sources include a number of intriguing ancient prophecies. These documents indicate that the time we are now living was to be the most pivotal era in the history of humanity. From approximately 1989–2012 humankind would undergo a radical shift in consciousness, an unprecedented shift never before experienced in our world. Mysteries would be revealed that conveyed how life operates at the most fundamental level, allowing us to live in a way never before imagined. Answers to our innermost prayers for a 'magic pill,' a panacea that would enable us to heal the ills of humankind would finally be known. Sound incredible? Exciting?

But what if that information threatened what we now believe? What if that 'magic pill' wasn't a pill at all?

What if some of our fundamental assumptions about life were actually wrong? So wrong, they have led us down a path fraught with illness, divorce, racism, poverty, heartache, crime, and all the other afflictions that have long plagued humankind. Next item to consider: How would this new information be imparted? Was someone appointed to impart it? Moreover, if someone actually purported to be aware of this new, more expansive version of 'truth,' would we take them seriously? Probably not.

So, what would it take to awaken humanity to new evolutionary knowledge? What would it take to capture the attention of the entire world to the degree that a radical shift in consciousness could occur?

An event of magnitude. An event so riveting that each of us would be shaken to our core and kicked out of our comfort zones.

I believe the September 11 attacks served as that event. A big-time 'wake-up call' was delivered to humanity on that fateful day; a 9-1-1 emergency call sent that was intended to trigger the shift in consciousness the Ancients spoke of.

Why did we need to wake up? Well, that is exactly what this book is about for there are many reasons. So, now that our attention has been captured, now that we've been thrust from our comfort zones and find ourselves shivering in the cold, are we willing to look deeper and uncover the reasons?

"Something we were withholding made us weak.
Until we found it was ourselves."

— ROBERT FROST
1874-1963

The largest obstacle facing the human race is 'us;' our reluctance to explore that which lies outside of our comfort zones. So the question I pose to you is: Are you willing to explore new territories..., even if they challenge what you now believe? Did the events of September 11 evoke a resolve within you to uncover the underlying causes of these tragedies so that we can avert future disasters?

"And the day came when the risk to remain tight
in the bud was more painful than the risk it took
to blossom."

— ANÄIS NIN
1903-1977

"Our ordinary consciousness filters out [an]
awareness of this mysterious, enlarged dimension,
yet until we have come to terms with its existence
we must beware lest we make a 'premature
foreclosure on reality'."

— MARILYN FERGUSON
The Aquarian Conspiracy - pg 48

"The most beautiful thing we can experience is
the mysterious. It is the source of all true art and
science. He to whom this emotion is a stranger,
who can no longer pause to wonder and stand
rapt in awe, is as good as dead: His eyes are
closed."

— ALBERT EINSTEIN
1879-1955

"What we have to do is be forever curiously testing new opinions and courting new impressions. The important thing is to not stop questioning. Curiosity has its own reason for existing. One cannot help but be in awe when he contemplates the mysteries of the eternity of life, of the marvelous structure of reality. It is enough if one tries merely to comprehend a little of this mystery every day. Never lose a holy curiosity."
— ALBERT EINSTEIN
1879-1955

"Not knowing when the dawn will come, I open every door."
— EMILY DICKINSON
1830-1886

"Where there is an open mind, there will always be a frontier."
— CHARLES F. KETTERING
1876-1958

The answers we are seeking do not lie in one realm of life. They can only be found by integrating knowledge from many realms, including ancient prophecies, the mysterious Bible Code, as well as extraordinary information imparted in the Dead Sea Scrolls. And though each of the preceding realms could be thought of as simply 'interesting dinner table conversation,' it is when we connect these pieces of the 'puzzle of life' with others found in the science of Quantum Physics, that a compelling image begins to form before our eyes. An image suggesting that the ancient prophecies were something more than the rantings of delusional folks who had nothing better to do with their time but conjure farfetched stories.

Having connected these particular pieces of the 'puzzle of life,' I have come to believe that those who departed on September 11 did so for a reason — a noble reason; one that will not only catalyze the dawning of a magnificent future for humankind, but also help to alleviate much of the pain, anguish, and suffering that has been a part of our existence for such a long long time. But that is my truth, and now you must find your own.

> "'Open your eyes,' they were saying, 'there is more.' More depth, height, dimension, perspectives, choices than we had imagined... Throughout history there were lone individuals here and there, or small bands at the fringes of science or religion, who, based on their own experiences, believed that people might someday transcend narrow 'normal' consciousness and reverse the brutality and alienation of the human condition... They celebrated the freedom found in the larger context and warned of the dangerous blindness of the prevailing view. Long before global war, ecological stress, and nuclear crisis struck, they feared for the future of a people without a context. Although they themselves moved beyond the dominant ideas of their day, they carried few of their contemporaries with them. Most often they were misunderstood, lonely, even ostracized.... Their ideas, however, served as fuel for future generations."
>
> — MARILYN FERGUSON
> *The Aquarian Conspiracy - pp 45–46*

> *"Do not believe what you have heard. Do not believe in tradition because it is handed down many generations. Do not believe in anything that has been spoken of many times. Do not believe because the written statements come from some old sage. Do not believe in conjecture. Do not believe in authority or teachers or elders. But after careful observations and analysis, when it agrees with reason and it will benefit one and all, then accept it and live by it."*
>
> — THE BUDDHA

Let's now begin our exploration of the ideas left by those who dared to challenge the prevailing beliefs of humanity. My heart, and I believe the hearts of those who 'crossed over' on September 11, are with you as you begin to contemplate a more expansive version of reality. My innermost wish is to instill a new hope in your heart for the future, to assist you in some meaningful way along your journey, and to illuminate the higher purpose of September 11 so that three-thousand forty-four lives did not end prematurely in vain.

> *"If I can stop one heart from breaking, I shall not live in vain; if I can ease one life the aching, or cool one pain, or help one fainting robin into his nest again, I shall not live in vain."*
>
> — EMILY DICKINSON
> *1830-1886*

From my heart,

Lauren Tratar

 Table of Contents

CHAPTER III

Your Comfort Zone...57

CHAPTER IV

September 11: A 9-1-1 Emergency Call to Humankind?...63

CHAPTER V

The Shift of the Ages...73

CHAPTER VI

The Bible Code...91

CHAPTER VII

Quantum Physics...101

CHAPTER VIII

Life Prior to September 11...137

CHAPTER IV

Unveiling the "Mystery of Mysteries"...147

CHAPTER X

The Time Has Come to Advance Our Thoughts...153

CHAPTER XI

Geophysical Changes and Their Effects...169

CHAPTER XII

Arriving at a 'Soulution' Layer by Layer...175

CHAPTER XIII

Soulution Part I: Eradicating Terrorism: Old-Paradigm Force Versus New-Paradigm Power...181

CHAPTER XIV

Soulution Part II: Achieving Peace Through Authentic Power...201

CHAPTER XV

Soulution Part III: Self Confrontation: Cleaning up Our Own Backyard...213

CHAPTER XVI

Soulution Part IV: Living at the Next Level of Consciousness...221

CHAPTER XVII

Humankind at a Crossroads...229

Bibliography & Permissions...235

 INTRODUCTION

September 11, 2001
Another Day That Will Live in Infamy

*"Within the next ten years, America will have a
renaissance or a catastrophe. Something is going
to happen to take us back to who we are."*
— MARIANNE WILLIAMSON
The Healing of America (1997) - pg 33

The unthinkable, unspeakable, unconscionable
occurred on September 11, 2001. Deeply etched in
our consciousness are the images of planes crashing
into the World Trade Center Towers — scenes so
surreal they defied belief. These images were, in fact,
so unfathomable that when the first tower was struck,
we thought it was an accident. But when a second

plane tore into the second tower, a third sliced open the Pentagon, and a fourth crashed in the Pennsylvania countryside, we were aghast, dumbfounded. America was being attacked before our very eyes. On a beautiful autumn morning in September we were violated beyond our wildest imaginings. We no longer held the distinction of innocence. Never before had a generation witnessed first-hand something so graphic. Desensitized to the diabolic and profane through movies and television, we had difficulty grasping the reality of what we were seeing. It was beyond comprehension.

A blanket of fear then descended upon us. We were afraid to fly. After all, the terrorists used commercial jets to commit their acts of violence. The airline industry was put into a state of upheaval. Their bottom line, ascertained through past statistics, was now meaningless. Who could have forecast events of this magnitude?

Before we had time to process the horrors we had just witnessed, our attention was then wrested by the deadly bacteria Anthrax. The new targets? Those who held high official positions, as well as high-profile media anchors — anyone whose death might invoke terror in the hearts of Americans. But rather than reaching the intended targets, this lethal powder was instead killing those who handled the mail. Unsuspecting innocent people were dying, for a mere sniff of this potent substance was capable of killing in days. Even more frightening, we didn't have a clue as to who was responsible for these attacks.

Next, our economy was subjected to the ensuing domino-effect and took a hit — big-time. An already fragile stock market that was teetering before the attacks, was now toppling and threatening to paralyze our nation.

If that wasn't enough for our minds to handle, we were then subjected to the plight of the Afghan people, most notably the women; the beatings, executions, stripping them of jobs, schooling, or any form of dignity, reducing them to beggars, impotent to change anything under the most drastic of conditions.

"TO EVERY ACTION THERE IS AN EQUAL AND OPPOSITE REACTION"

Our minds could take no more. This confluence of events had thrust us into a state of 'input-overload.' We experienced such a emotional roller coaster, we were spent; exhausted. In one moment, we were inconsolable, feeling the gut-wrenching pain of those searching for their loved ones, and in the next, profoundly grateful for those who had risked their lives to save others. But our turbulent ride did not end there. As we witnessed our brothers and sisters around the world stand beside us and grieve our inexpressible loss in our greatest hour of need, we experienced yet another wave of intense emotion. The flag in Moscow, representing those who were once our archenemies, flew in compassion at half-mast. In an extraordinary moment of heartfelt emotion, the people of England sang our national anthem. People all over the world placed flowers outside the American embassies in an unprecedented display of sympathy never before experienced on this planet. In these moments, humanity was brought together, our brotherhood affirmed. The terrorists had not only struck the heart of America, but the heart of humankind. They crossed a line that most human beings felt to their core.

WHY, WHY, WHY?

"The search for truth is more precious than its possession."

— ALBERT EINSTEIN
1879-1955

After recoiling from these events we began our search for the 'why.' Why would others perpetrate such a hideous crime against *us* — innocent Americans? And though many television programs conveyed a great deal of information about Islam, terrorism, Bin-Laden's fifty-one brothers and sisters, flying school, karate, etc., they never quite uncovered the underlying reasons beyond the most simplistic. Responses such as: "The terrorists are jealous of the United States," "The Taliban is envious of our freedom," and "There is evil in the world that must be stamped out," didn't begin to scratch the surface of what we knew in our hearts to be a much more complex and multifaceted issue.

Instinctive to the human condition is the need for answers — meaningful answers. Answers provide relief, a form of certainty that allows us to move into the future with hope. Whenever we experience pain that wounds us deeply, or fear that frightens us intensely, we instinctively seek answers to diminish our pain. And regardless of where we place blame, we typically adapt a 'survival mechanism' to protect ourselves in the future. "If it happened once," we tell ourselves, "it could happen again." What we end up with, though, is 'excess baggage' — a myriad of defensive 'survival' reactions that get in the way of living life to the fullest: long check-in lines at the airport, extensive baggage searches, new bacteria-killing equipment in our post offices, etc. We will subject ourselves to all sorts of elaborate outward impositions to ensure our protection, but ordinarily won't go *inward* deep enough to uncover the 'core issue' — the issue *underlying* the event — the cause responsible for the effect. It's a game we've been playing for a long time, but this game must now end. September 11 demands it. The 3,044 people who perished on that fateful day deserve it.

If we fail to uncover the underlying issues that culminated in the September 11 attacks, if we prematurely close the chapter on these tragedies and chalk them up to 'random acts of terrorism,' if we sweep this issue under the rug and simply adapt more and more 'survival mechanisms,' we will be doing ourselves a great disservice. For we will then be forced to repeat this 'lesson' *until* we understand why it occurred. No thank you. I, for one, have seen enough pain and cried enough tears.

> *"Those who do not learn from history, are doomed to repeat it."*
> — UNKNOWN

Just as a child will do many things to get his parents attention, some we might consider as 'evil,' the same is true of unexamined, unresolved core issues. Why? A powerful law of nature guarantees it; a law you will soon become familiar with, for it not only lies at the core of these tragedies, but also happens to be shaping your every moment.

Deep in our hearts most of us want to believe that everything happens for a reason — that nothing in life is an accident, or simply coincidental. But if there are no coincidences, what does that say about what we currently know about life? If the September 11 attacks, the massive job layoffs, the declining economy, and widespread fear that accompanies such circumstances actually have a greater meaning, what could that meaning be?

WHAT QUALIFIES ME TO BE THE HARBINGER OF THIS NEWS?

> *"You cannot know who is going to bring you your future. You cannot qualify them in advance by looking at degrees or experience, or gender, or race. You can only LISTEN."*
> — JOEL ARTHUR BARKER
> *Paradigms: The Business of Discovering the Future - pg 70*

I am not worthy, I am not worthy, I am not worthy….and so the mantra goes. But as fate would have it, I find myself in the unique position of perhaps shedding light on this subject. From 1996 through mid-2000, I conducted extensive research for a book I was writing entitled *LIFE: A Complete Operating Manual* (subtitle) *The Secret to Life Unveiled: Who You Really Are, How Life Really Operates, and How to Unleash the Incredible Power Within!*. And though *"Life"* was released in January 2001, I 'coincidentally' never stopped my research. The knowledge I acquired, in my estimation, provides an entirely new perspective on these tragic events — one that has not yet been touched on. At the heart of *"Life"* is a premise that has been written about for millennia: "Your thoughts create your reality." And though that premise may seem mystical and fanciful to some, I promise you, it is not.

To establish its veracity, I painstakingly incorporated a great quantity of 'evidence' in the form of 1,105 quotations from a myriad of diverse sources: quantum physics, ancient teachings, current medical knowledge, spirituality, philosophy, and metaphysics, and wove them into a cohesive comprehensive tapestry. Amazingly, I found that each of these sources contributed a piece to the 'puzzle of life' that happened to dovetail together and form an incredible image — one that revealed a more expansive reality, a reality that supersedes our current reality!

Compelling evidence of the power of thought is found in many documents, old and new. Two thousand five hundred-year-old texts, entitled *The Essene Gospels of Peace*, were discovered in the secret archives of the Vatican Library by Edmond Szekely in the early 1920's. Fragments of identical documents were also found in the Dead Sea Scrolls in 1947 — originals of many texts that were utilized in the Bible. Astonishingly, these documents contain numerous references to the power of thought:

> *"For to no other creature in the kingdom of our Earthly mother is given the power of thought. All the beasts that crawl and birds that fly live not of their own thinking but of a law that governs all life. Only to the sons and daughters of man is given the power of thought. And even that thought can break the bonds of death. Do not think that because it cannot be seen that thought has no power, for I'll tell you truly that the lightning that cleaves the mighty oak, the quaking the opens up cracks in the earth, these are like the play of children compared to the power of your thought."*
> — THE ESSENE GOSPEL OF PEACE - BOOK 4
> *The Teachings of the Elect - pg 32*

I spent most of 2001 promoting *"Life,"* speaking at bookstores, seminars, exhibiting at the BookExpo America show, and talking the ear off of just about anyone who would listen. (Most were kind and put up with me…). While engaged in these activities, I met people who were very interested in my work because it offered rational answers to that which is seemingly irrational. As a result, my phone began to ring shortly after the terrorist attacks occurred. Those yearning to make sense of this tragedy were curious to hear my insights: Did I feel there was a higher purpose in what had occurred? And that is what compelled me to pen my thoughts.

From what I have learned about the power of thought and how it functions, I must, at the least, attempt to shed some light on this dilemma. Like so many who felt an inner urgency to help, I too, must *do* something.

My intent is to provide inspiration and hope for our future. But rather than simply imparting words of wisdom, I propose a tangible solution to the quandary we now face, as well as the means to attain it utilizing the greatest power ever bestowed to humankind: Thought. For what good is all the esoteric inspirational knowledge in the world if it can't be used to make life better, easier, or more enjoyable, right? And if nothing else, after reading this book, you will know how to harness the extraordinary power of your thoughts to heal your life, our nation, and the world.

So if you're ready to explore the higher purpose of September 11 and become acquainted with your authentic power, buckle up, for you *will* be leaving your comfort zone. I will present ideas that you are probably unfamiliar with, which may feel a bit unsettling. But rather than passing premature judgement and "throwing the baby out with the bath water," I ask that you temporarily accompany me to a place that Rumi, a Persian Sufi poet, spoke of in the 1200s. He said:

> *"There is a field beyond right and wrong. I will meet you there."*

I ask you to meet me in a place of neutrality because your Western orientation to life has conditioned you to filter information through logic and rational thought alone, to be skeptical of anything that deviates from what you now know. Consequently, your logical mind needs to be shown, actually convinced beyond a doubt through compelling evidence, that everything in life is totally and completely interlinked, or it will mete judgement from a narrow perspective — its comfort zone.

> *"The brain chooses between conflicting views. It represses information that does not fit with its dominant beliefs. Unless, of course, it can harmonize the ideas into a powerful synthesis."*
> — MARILYN FERGUSON
> *The Aquarian Conspiracy - pg 72*

I ask that you explore this information with an open mind and innocent perception so your mind and heart *together* can perceive that which is beyond the obvious — the surface issues — and begin to contemplate what lies deeper.

To present this complex issue in a cohesive manner, it is essential that you have a basis of understanding. Because the brain is somewhat like a biocomputer, information must be 'downloaded' in a specific, sequential 'connect-the-dots' manner or it will simply shut down. For example, before compre-hending geometry, you required the knowledge of arithmetic, right? Unlike a computer though, the brain goes further. For if it is given information it cannot process, i.e., does not make sense, it will try to locate the *cause* of its distress and then engage in one of two responses. Instinctively it will either "flee," throw the baby out with the bath water, or "fight," engage in a 'search and destroy mission,' blame or find fault with whatever makes logical sense. And because I am presenting this information, guess who is the likely target? Therefore, to avoid slinging arrows fired at me, and to satisfy your left-brain's need for information, the first part of this book will be devoted to providing a basis of understanding. In the second, we will utilize that knowledge to explore a new-paradigm solution to the quandary presented by September 11.

Acknowledging the formidable task in front of me, I will present my 'case,' item by item, as an attorney might deliver a case to a jury. Be advised though: some of my witnesses and evidence are not 'provable' in a scientific sense. Quite intentionally, I have interspersed quotations from metaphysical sources (that which is incapable of being verified with your physical senses). Among these sources is the best-selling series of books entitled *Conversations with God*, by Neale Donald Walsch. Now I realize that such an ambiguous source may raise eyebrows, but my intent is to stimulate both your left and right-brain comprehension, which will allow you to perhaps recontextualize some of your old ideas into a more expansive framework. Furthermore, if you are able to maintain an innocent perception, which may be challenging, your logical mind will then begin to merge with your heart and new doors will open. For true power lies in the *integration* of your mind and heart. I might also add that Albert Einstein said:

> *"The more I study physics, the more I am drawn to metaphysics."*
>
> — ALBERT EINSTEIN

To begin, it is essential that you acknowledge that we, as humankind, although brilliant in many areas, do not have all the answers. And to take it a step further, some of the 'truths' we now take for granted may be outmoded, needing to be replaced by a more expansive version of truth, for truth is an ever-evolving aspect of life.

> *"The idea that truth is not absolute and forever, but a function of a particular time and place, has been slowly gaining ground and power for almost two hundred years. It can be seen in the ideas of Bergson, Marx, Darwin, Einstein — to name but a few of the early giants of this way of thinking."*
>
> — RUBEN NELSON
> *Reflections on Paradigms - 1993*
> *a paper prepared for The Environment Council of Alberta, Canada*

In *Conversations with God* it was conveyed that we must question what we now deem as truth:

> *"Go ahead and act on all that you know [now].*
> *But notice that you've all been doing that since*
> *time began. And look at what shape the world is*
> *in. Clearly, you've missed something. Obviously,*
> *there is something you don't understand. That*
> *which you do understand may seem right to you,*
> *because 'right' is a term you use to designate*
> *something with which you agree. What you've*
> *missed will, therefore, appear at first to be*
> *'wrong.' The only way to move forward on this*
> *is to ask yourself, 'What would actually happen*
> *if everything I thought was 'wrong' was actually*
> *'right'?' Every great scientist knows about this.*
> *When what a scientist does is not working, a*
> *scientist sets aside all assumptions and starts*
> *over. All great discoveries have been made from*
> *a willingness, and ability, to not be right. And*
> *that's what's needed here."*
> — NEALE DONALD WALSCH
> *Conversations with God - Book 1 - pg 7*

Throughout this discourse I will remind you of the need to remain open, to maintain an innocent perception, for I realize this is difficult — the antithesis of a knee-jerk 'preprogrammed' reaction to that which you do not yet comprehend. However, to understand why our world is in the shape it is in, and why the catastrophe of September 11 took place, we must look beneath the surface layers of life, beneath our societal paradigms — how we as a culture, subcultures, families, etc., currently view life.

To solve the mystery of September 11, and that of life itself, a number of clues have been passed onto us throughout the ages. And quite a few were contributed by our friend Albert Einstein who said:

> *"Problems cannot be solved at the same level of awareness that created them."*

So, it appears that solutions to problems lie at the *next* level of awareness. Dr. Einstein also cautioned:

> *"We shall require a substantially new manner of thinking if mankind is to survive."*

Okay, what does that mean? Stay tuned and you'll find out, for that admonition is significant.

Now that your appetite has been whetted, your curiosity piqued, let's dive into the 'meat' of this discourse. In short, I intend to present evidence that suggests that the September 11 events actually had a *number* of purposes — some evident, and others that require a deeper examination.

THE HIGHER PURPOSES OF SEPTEMBER 11

1) *TO ALERT US TO THE GROWTH AND THREAT OF TERRORISM* — a cancer must be treated, its source illuminated and then healed, for it is posing a formidable threat to life, liberty, and the pursuit of happiness in our world

2) *TO ILLUMINATE ATROCITIES* occurring in our world that require our aid and assistance

3) *TO SPAWN UNITY* — to open our eyes and hearts to the numerous commonalities we share with seemingly dissimilar others, thereby facilitating a newfound understanding of our interconnectedness

4) *TO CATALYZE THE COLLECTIVE EVOLUTION* of humankind into the next level of consciousness

5) *TO ALERT US TO A GRAVE DANGER* now posed to humankind. This threat requires our immediate attention for it is creating a barrier to our evolution

While the first three items on this list compelled us to take immediate action, the last two have heretofore gone unnoticed. In my estimation, they are the most significant reasons that a 9-1-1 emergency call was placed to humankind — a call we may soon recognize as a gift beyond measure.

With no further ado, let's begin building our foundation of understanding so that we are able to contemplate both the higher purpose of the grievous events that occurred on September 11, 2001, and life itself, from a place of heightened awareness.

CHAPTER 1

Looking at Life From a Higher Perspective

"*A single thread in a tapestry, though its color brightly shines, can never see its purpose in the pattern of the grand design... So how can you know what your life is worth or where your value lies? You can never see through the eyes of man. You must look at your life through Heaven's Eyes.*"

— STEVEN SCHWARTZ

"Through Heaven's Eyes" from the motion picture "The Prince of Egypt"

Songwriters are said to be the prophets of time. And the time we are now living is no exception. One of the most preeminent and gifted songwriters today is Steven Schwartz, whose body of work speaks volumes of his 'connection' to something 'otherworldly.' In one of the beautiful songs he wrote for the motion picture *"Prince of Egypt,"* Steven explains that we will never understand life unless we view it from a higher, more expansive perspective — through "Heaven's Eyes."

So, to uncover the higher purpose of the September 11 attacks, we must first expand our perspective and consider the 'bigger picture' of life. For without knowledge of the 'bigger picture,' viewing life through Heaven's eyes, nothing can or will make sense.

A MASTER PLAN?

Intimations of a higher purpose underlying these tragedies — a purpose that lies at another level of awareness — were rampant immediately following September 11. Many victims' loved ones expressed a 'knowingness' that these tragedies had a higher purpose. And though psychologists might argue that those responses were simply a 'survival' reaction to the extreme nature of this event, that response would simply expose *their* paradigm — what they have come to believe through years of study. And again, the purpose of this discourse is to consider what is *underlying* commonly held paradigms, to look beneath what we now deem as truth. I have come to believe that when one is in a state of raw uncensored emotion, not filtered through logic but the heart, one 'knows' far more than what we currently assume.

One of the many heroes of September 11 was a chaplain from a New York City firehouse. Perhaps you heard the heart-warming, heart-wrenching story of the Franciscan Catholic priest, Father Mychal Judge. Father Mychal was a revered fellow among his peers, a pillar of strength who always provided words of solace for his comrades when they had difficulty coping with the numerous tragedies a firefighter is exposed to day after day. Upon hearing the news of the Trade Center disaster, Father Mychal hastily removed his chaplain habit and donned his firefighter gear. When his battalion arrived at the scene of devastation, Father Mychal was needed immediately. As fate would have it, while administering the last rites to an unfortunate victim, Father Mychal was struck by a piece of falling debris which killed him instantly. Shortly after his funeral services, a fellow firefighter explained to the media that Father Mychal was needed on the 'other side' to assist his dear friends and others who were then 'crossing over.' Although grief-stricken by the loss of their beloved chaplain, Father Mychal had endowed his 'brothers' with many gifts — insights which allowed them to view his death "Through Heaven's Eyes." He had always explained that every event, regardless of how horrific it was, was all a part of God's 'Master Plan.'

Could there be a Master Plan? And if so, how could it include such an atrocity? To understand this paradox, we must address the perennial question:

"What are we doing here on Planet Earth?"

THE SCHOOLROOM NAMED EARTH

"Life is a succession of lessons which must be lived to be understood."

— HELEN KELLER
1880-1968

"The purpose of time is to enable you to learn how to use time constructively. It is thus a teaching device and a means to an end. Time will cease when it is no longer useful in facilitating learning."

— A COURSE IN MIRACLES®
pg 4

"We don't receive wisdom, we must discover it for ourselves after a journey that no one can take for us or spare us."

— MARCEL PROUST
1871-1922

Throughout the ages, spiritual teachers have instructed that Life on Earth is a course of experience we must go through in order to graduate to higher levels of being. If that's the case, what are we here to learn?

I believe that each of us has our own unique Master Plan detailing what we are to learn, and that we, as humankind, also have a Master Plan. And though each of our plans differs in their specifics, each shares the same objective: *Evolution* — the expansion or advancement of our souls through experience.

THE CURRICULUM: EVOLUTION

"Life is a maze in which we take the wrong turning before we have learned to walk."
— CYRIL CONNOLLY
1903-1974

"Evolution, innate to the overall field of consciousness, guarantees the salvation of mankind, and with it, all of life."
— DR. DAVID HAWKINS
Power Versus Force - pg 92

"There are no mistakes, no coincidences. All events are blessings given to us to learn from."
— ELIZABETH KÜBLER-ROSS

"The hard knocks we receive from bounding like a pinball between life's extremes, beyond the outer limits of our comfort zone, are our greatest teachers. They let us know when we're off course, teach us discrimination, stretch our abilities and capacities. All antagonisms are complementary and ultimately serve life's purpose."
— MOIRA TIMMS
Beyond Prophecies and Predictions - pg 13

Have you ever noticed that evolution occurs, both personally and collectively, whether you know it or not? Think about it. Do you know more today than you did ten years ago? Have you grown wiser from the experiences of your life? Probably.

Now let's take that premise a step further. Have we, as humankind, not experienced incredible growth during the past one hundred years? I think you'll agree that evolution has occurred. In fact, it is inevitable, it happens with or without our conscious awareness.

SPIRAL DYNAMICS

"The main obstacle to man's development is his lack of knowledge about the nature of consciousness itself."
— DR. DAVID HAWKINS
Power Versus Force - pg 21

Further evidence of evolution being the objective of the 'Master Plan' is derived from author Ken Wilber in *A Theory of Everything*. Contributing a significant piece to the 'puzzle of life,' Wilber contends that the knowledge of "Spiral Dynamics" is essential in order to comprehend the 'bigger picture' of life. Spiral Dynamics, a concept authored by researchers Christopher Cowan and Don Beck, is a refinement of developmental psychology — the study of the growth and development of the mind which examines the dynamics of consciousness. In principle, more than one hundred different research studies testing more than fifty thousand people across the globe, have agreed on one item: The development of consciousness occurs in a series of unfolding stages. Spiral Dynamics asserts that eight different stages of development, referred to as *memes,* exist in humanity, and that every person on the face of this planet is engaged in one of those memes. In somewhat the same manner that schools are separated into various grade levels, the same is true of the consciousness of humankind. Eighth-graders have had more experience, and thus have greater cognitive capacity than second-graders, right? Since each differs in the amount of experience they have undergone, each holds a different level of consciousness commensurate with that level of experience. The same is true of memes. Each meme simply represents a different level of experience, hence a different level of consciousness.

How is this knowledge useful in everyday life? Mr. Cowan and Mr. Beck have actually applied this information in South Africa where they were asked to help resolve the longstanding race issue — apartheid. Through their knowledge of Spiral Dynamics, they have recognized that, at its essence, racism is not about skin color but disparities in memes.

Each meme has its own belief system and unique set of attributes which has a dominant influence on an individual's comfort zone. The dynamics of a specific meme are, in fact, so deeply ingrained in a person's consciousness that he or she will fervently defend the merits of that meme as being the 'one and only': "My beliefs are right, yours are wrong, and if I can't force you to see the err of your ways, I must protect the world from 'your kind' or it will go to hell!" The old 'save the world from evil' story that has been told, retold, and embellished on throughout the ages.

> *"The truth of each level of consciousness is self-verifying, in that each level has its native range of perception which confirms what is already believed to be true. Thus, everyone feels justified in the viewpoints which underlie his actions and beliefs."*
>
> — DR. DAVID HAWKINS
> *Power Versus Force - pg 21*

All eight memes exist in this schoolroom called Earth, which is essential, for when we complete the lessons in one meme, when we can see its pros and cons from an unbiased perspective, we will instinctively be drawn to the next. Now this phase of transition is not necessarily 'fun,' because we must then regain our 'centers' and find a new level of comfort as we make our way through a whole new set of beliefs — a daunting task. However, as we move closer and closer to the next meme, a helping hand will typically be extended from someone who has 'been there and done that,' one who will offer words of wisdom, comfort, and encouragement.

Wilber also conveys interesting information in light of September 11, for he contends that approximately Eighty Million people are now on the threshold of making a momentous leap into the highest levels of consciousness. These higher memes, heretofore populated by few, are characterized by a holistic integral approach to life, attributes that transcend the 'one and only meme' position, understanding the contribution that each meme provides to the whole. Wilber states that it is now critical that this leap in consciousness occurs, for if it does not:

"...humanity will be destined to remain victims of a global 'autoimmune disease' where various memes turn on each other in an attempt to establish supremacy." pg 14

The knowledge of Spiral Dynamics offers an invaluable perspective, one that is essential in understanding our fellow students, because the "health of the whole," all of us that comprise humankind, is *dependent* on all eight memes existing simultaneously. All memes *must* exist for choice and evolution to occur, for where would we evolve to if the next meme was not available? And, how much fun would life be if we lived in a sea of sameness, a place where everyone thought the same things, held the same beliefs, looked identical, and behaved in the exact same manner? In other words, would you *want* to live in a world populated by six Billion 'yous'?

OUR COLLECTIVE EVOLUTION

"Every few hundred years in Western history there occurs a sharp transformation. Within a few short decades, society — its world view, its basic values, its social and political structures, its arts, its key institutions — rearranges itself. And the people born then cannot even imagine a world in which their grandparents lived and into which their own parents were born. We are currently living through such a transformation."
— PETER DRUCKER
Post-Capitalist Society

*"Sooner or later, if human society is to evolve —
indeed, if it is to survive — we must match our
two lives to our new knowledge. For too long, the
Two Cultures — the esthetic, feeling humanities
and cool, analytical science — have functioned
independently, like the right and left
hemispheres of a split-brain patient. We have
been the victims of our collective divided
consciousness."*

— MARILYN FERGUSON
The Aquarian Conspiracy - pg 187

Now that you have a more expansive understanding
of an individual's process of evolution, let's delve
into our collective evolution, for once more,
evolution is the objective of life. In order for
humanity, the macrocosm, as well as an individual,
the microcosm, to evolve, *every* aspect of our being
must evolve concurrently, for we are a triune being
composed of body, mind, and spirit. Therefore, if
we're evolving more rapidly in the technological and
scientific arena, the mind, and lagging in our spiritual
growth, an imbalance will result.

How do we regain our equilibrium? Sadly, at this
stage of our collective evolution, the only effective
means of alerting us to an imbalance is through
adversity — an important reason to uncover the
higher purpose of September 11. So let's now move
onto another important piece of the 'puzzle of life'
— the higher purpose of adversity — for
understanding that premise sheds even more light on
the atrocities of September 11.

CHAPTER II

Adversity Catalyzes Evolution

"I wake up shivering from horror's still too fresh in my mind. Why must darkness precede the dawn? Why is death the prerequisite to life? I rub my eyes open. The long night is ended now. The first rays of a new dawn illuminate my path, beckoning me to follow. Can I shape the following day?"

— KIARA WINDRIDER

"There are some things you learn best in calm, and some in storm."

— WILLA CATHER
1873-1947

"A single event can awaken within us a stranger previously unknown to us."

— ANTOINE DE SAINT-EXUPERY
1900-1944

"Conflict, pain, tension, fear, paradox.... these are transformations trying to happen. Once we confront them, the transformative process begins. Those who discover this phenomenon, whether by search or accident, gradually realize that the reward is worth the scariness of unanesthetized life. The release of pain, the sense of liberation, and the resolution of conflict make the next crisis or stubborn paradox easier to confront."

— MARILYN FERGUSON
The Aquarian Conspiracy - pg 76

"Anything that disrupts the old order of our lives has the potential for triggering a transformation, a movement toward greater maturity, openness, strength."

— MARILYN FERGUSON
The Aquarian Conspiracy - pg 73

Why do we require something as dreadful as adversity, crisis, or disaster in order to evolve? As you can clearly see in the wake of September 11, adversity is a 'wake-up' call. Adversity forces us to examine what is *truly* important in life — to explore areas we may have denied, overlooked, or deemed inconsequential. Adversity creates a contraction that impels expansion, it produces a degeneration that induces regeneration. Adversity provides definitive moments that catalyze a turning point in life, moments that compel us to reach beyond the pain we are experiencing and seek a new direction. Adversity implores us to examine the 'bigger picture' and ask penetrating questions: *"Where are we,"* and more important, *"Where are we going?"* For if we discover that our path is headed in the wrong direction, we have the opportunity to alter its course before it's too late.

THE EVOLUTION OF EBENEZER SCROOGE

"Out of every crisis comes the chance to be reborn, to reconceive ourselves as individuals, to choose the kind of change that will help us to grow and to fulfill ourselves more completely."
— NENA O'NEILL

"Most people don't know there are angels whose only job is to make sure you don't get too comfortable and fall asleep and miss your life."
— BRIAN ANDREAS
Still Mostly True

Consider the story of Ebenezer Scrooge in Dicken's classic, *A Christmas Carol*. Mr. Scrooge was a nasty unkind old man who didn't care a lick about others. He was stuck in a rut, safely inside his comfort zone, when suddenly, one night while deep in sleep, ghosts appeared and provided him a big-time 'Reality Check' — a view of his life through 'Heaven's eyes.' As Mr. Scrooge examined the repercussions of his tyrannical ways from this higher perspective, he was able to awaken a dormant sense of love, appreciation, and compassion for others within. *Only* through this frightening experience was he able to gain insights that impelled him to change his life forever. *Where was he* and *where was he going* before adversity came knocking at his door?

"THE GAME"

"Pain exists to promote evolution; its cumulative effect finally forces us in a new direction."
— DR. DAVID HAWKINS
Power Versus Force - pg 104

Another example of adversity spawning evolution was seen in the movie, *"The Game,"* starring Michael Douglas. This movie effectively illustrated how adversity gives birth to new perspectives that open the door for evolution to occur.

Motivated primarily by greed and conquest, the character Mr. Douglas portrayed had created a formidable business empire largely by taking advantage of those less fortunate. He had become a cold, hardened man, oblivious to the plight of others. Alarmed by his distressing change in character, those formerly close to him were compelled to take dramatic action. His younger brother purchased an unforgettable birthday gift for him, an experience labeled "The Adventure of a Lifetime" — a kind of 'rich man's intervention.' When Mr. Douglas' character agreed to participate in this adventure, he had no idea what was in store for him. A very real drama ensued, one that forced him into circumstances that seemingly jeopardized his life. However, as he overcame adversity after adversity, each calling on hidden sources of strength and awareness, he was able to uncover a buried love and compassion that lay dormant within his heart. At the conclusion of his very real drama, when he realized *where he was* and *where he was going*, a new man was born within. A new dimension of his soul emerged, a dimension that included a newly-found appreciation for life, love, and purpose.

HAVE THE SEPTEMBER 11 TRAGEDIES SPAWNED CHANGE?

"Only that which is deeply felt can change us. Rational arguments alone cannot penetrate the layers of fear and conditioning that comprise our crippling belief systems."
— MARILYN FERGUSON
The Aquarian Conspiracy - pg 35

"Crises do not represent breakdown, but break-through in advancing the human community."
— THE WHOLE EARTH PAPERS

Looking back on the events of 9-11, have we changed? Undeniably, in the short-term. Life on Monday, September 10 was vastly different from life on Tuesday. Consider the following email I received from an unknown author:

On Monday there were people who fought against praying in schools.

On Tuesday you would have been hard pressed to find a school where people were not praying.

On Monday there were people who separated one another by race, sex, color and creed.

On Tuesday, people, from all races, creeds, and religions, held hands.

On Monday there were people who thought of heroes as athletes.

On Tuesday people learned what the word hero really meant.

On Monday there were people who argued with their kids about picking up their rooms.

On Tuesday the same people could not get home fast enough to hug their kids.

On Monday there were people who became upset if their dry cleaning wasn't ready on time.

On Tuesday the same people lined up to give blood.

Where were we on Monday and where were we going? The larger question now posed to us is: Will the events of September 11 contribute to a *long-term* change in humanity?

❧

Shortly after the tragedies occurred, I received another email I'd like to share (I paraphrased a bit) by author Max Lucardo. He explains that although we are being asked to 'return to normal' we must ask ourselves, "Is that what we *really* want?"

"IS THIS NORMAL?"

Four thousand gathered for midday prayer in a downtown (New York) cathedral.

A New York City church, filled and emptied six times last Tuesday.

The owner of a Manhattan tennis shoe store threw open his doors and gave running shoes to those fleeing the towers.

People stood in lines to give blood, in hospitals to treat the sick, in sanctuaries to pray for the wounded.

America was different this week.

We wept for people we didn't know.

We sent money to families we've never seen.

Talk-show hosts read Scriptures, journalists printed prayers.

Our focus shifted from fashion hemlines and box scores to orphans and widows and the future of the world.

We were different this week.

Republicans stood next to Democrats.

Catholics prayed with Jews.

Skin color was covered by the ash of burning towers.

This country is different than it was a week ago.

We're not as self-centered as we were.

We're not as self-reliant as we were.

Hands are out; knees are bent.

This is not normal.

And I have to ask the question; 'Do we want to go back to normal?' Are we being given a glimpse of a new way of life? Are we, as a nation, being reminded that the enemy is not each other, the power is not in ourselves, and the future is not in our bank accounts? Could this unselfish prayerfulness be the way God intended for us to live all along? Maybe this, in His eyes, is the way we are called to live.

Perhaps we should follow the example of those on flight 93. Minutes before the fourth plane crashed in the fields of Pennsylvania, those on board devised a scheme. In a concerted harrowing effort, a few brave souls overcame the highjackers and averted the plane before it struck its intended Washington, D.C. target, thus saving the lives of countless innocent others. Before taking this courageous action, the heroes of Flight 93 phoned their loved ones and explained that they had become aware of the intent of the hijackers and had to do something about it.

We can do something as well. And perhaps the best response to this tragedy is to refuse to go back to normal.

— MAX LUCARDO

꩜

In moments of unity never before experienced on Earth, the events of Tuesday, September 11, ignited a new sense of community, compassion, love, brotherhood, and recognition of our inter-dependence. And perhaps even more occurred that we were unable to see — shifts in individual consciousness. For in a crisis it is common for habitual beliefs, judgments, and subconscious reactions to rise to the forefront and be forever changed. The result? *Evolution:* the objective of life.

"Tolerance for pain may be high, but it is not without limit. Eventually everyone begins to recognize, however dimly, that there must be a better way. As this recognition becomes more firmly established, it becomes a turning point."

— A COURSE IN MIRACLES®
pg 22

ADVANCE WARNINGS
ALWAYS PRECEDE CATASTROPHE

Before a large-scale disaster occurs, smaller adverse incidents always precede the crisis. These smaller incidents are 'wrong-way' signs, designed to warn us of impending disaster, providing us the opportunity to resolve an underlying imbalance in our beings. Unaware of their true purpose, we usually don't take action until something decisive pushes us over the edge — information echoed by author Joel Barker in *Paradigms: The Business of Discovering the Future.* Barker explains that a paradigm will not shift (change or evolution will not occur) *unless* there is discomfort or dissonance in the current paradigm — information also affirmed by Ken Wilber. Adversity provides that discomfort; it pushes us out of our comfort zones and impels us to look deeper. Keep in mind though, a large-scale catastrophe is simply the result of earlier warnings that have gone unheeded and will *only* occur when all other prior attempts to alert us to an imbalance in our beings have failed.

Why are we so reluctant to resolve our smaller problems? We've learned to accept them; they are part of our societal paradigm, considered "the twists and turns of fate." We've been 'programmed' to believe that having a multitude of issues is 'normal.' Our travails and tribulations have become our water cooler conversations, the topics of support groups, the reasons to spend endless hours on the phone commiserating with one another. Problems and their lack of meaningful resolution are part of our larger belief system, and therefore, fit neatly inside our comfort zones — regardless of how uncomfortable they may be.

As you're beginning to see, much transpired 'under the covers' that led to the events of September 11. However, to fully understand why these events occurred we would have to be playing the 'Game of Life' with a 'full deck.' But we're not. And our attempt to play this game without all the cards has resulted in chaos, confusion, pain, and anguish. Therefore, it is now time that we become cognizant of the missing cards, which I will unveil throughout this discourse so that you have all the knowledge and tools required to navigate the waters of life — calm or rough.

Lest you think it incredulous that we are currently not operating on all cylinders, remember, truth is an ever-evolving aspect of life. This implies that we are continually learning and fine-tuning, that our current truths will one day be replaced by a more expansive truth. To remind you of that fact, I will reiterate the following quotation from *Conversations with God*:

> "Go ahead and act on all that you know [now]. But notice that you've all been doing that since time began. And look at what shape the world is in. Clearly, you've missed something. Obviously, there is something you don't understand. That which you do understand may seem right to you, because 'right' is a term you use to designate something with which you agree. What you've missed will, therefore, appear at first to be 'wrong.' The only way to move forward on this is to ask yourself, 'What would actually happen if everything I thought was 'wrong' was actually

'right'?' Every great scientist knows about this.
When what a scientist does is not working, a
scientist sets aside all assumptions and starts
over. All great discoveries have been made from
a willingness, and ability, to not be right. And
that's what's needed here."

— NEALE DONALD WALSCH
Conversations with God - Book 1 - pg 7

"It is only when people begin to shake loose from
their preconceptions, from the ideas that have
dominated them, that we begin to receive a sense
of opening, a sense of vision."

— DAME BARBARA MARY WARD
1914-1981

"It is impossible for a man to learn what he
thinks he already knows."

— EPICTETUS
50-138 AD

"The most fatal illusion is the settled point of
view. Since life is growth and motion, a fixed
point of view kills anybody who has one."

— BROOKS ATKINSON
1894-1984

Let's now become acquainted with another important
piece of the 'puzzle of life:' our comfort zones. For
the knowledge of our comfort zones is essential in
understanding our evolution and ultimately why, I
believe, a 9-1-1 emergency call was placed to
mankind. I must warn you in advance though, your
comfort zone may begin to feel a bit uncomfortable
when we shine a bright light on all those 'skeletons'
lurking behind the closet doors.

CHAPTER III

Your Comfort Zone

"Be open. Don't close off the possibility of a new truth because you have been comfortable with an old one. Life begins at the end of your comfort zone."

— NEALE DONALD WALSCH
Conversations with God - Book 3 - pg 90

Your comfort zone is the synthesis of your belief system, societal paradigms, the meme you are engaged in, the culmination of your experiences, and the 'truth' *as you perceive it* from your unique perspective — the rules you live your life by. How was it created?

From the moment you were able to understand, your 'programming' began. Your primary caretakers 'taught you the ropes:' "This is good, that is bad, this is right, and that is wrong. If you do what is good and right you will be rewarded, but if you do what is bad and wrong, you will be punished." After acquiring the foundation of your comfort zone from your primary caretakers, the schools and society took over with their brand of rights, wrongs, etc., until you were fully 'downloaded' — your beliefs paralleled the majority of those around you. And though you didn't *consciously* choose to believe what you were taught, you adopted the majority of these prevailing beliefs and while doing so, created your comfort zone, and, incidentally, your life along with it. It is important to note as we move forward: This 'programming' differs from culture to culture, family to family, meme to meme, person to person.

> *"For the most part, [your judgments, decisions, and assessments] are decisions made not by you, but by someone else. Your parents, perhaps. Your religion. Your teachers, historians, politicians. Very few of the value judgments you have incorporated into your truth are judgments you, yourself, have made based on your own experience... You have created yourself out of the experience of others."*
>
> — NEALE DONALD WALSCH
> *Conversations with God - Book 1 - pg 62*

> *"Common sense is the collection of prejudices acquired by age eighteen."*
>
> — ALBERT EINSTEIN
> *1879-1955*

"To increase the power of human understanding, [we must] get under the surface of human life to consider the inherited and taken-for-granted sources of thought and action which underlie any given human culture or subculture... An understanding is sought which is deeper, more inclusive, more powerful, more conscious, and hence, more reliable, than are the surface understandings of our immediate experience."

— RUBEN NELSON
Reflections on Paradigms - 1993
a paper prepared for The Environment Council of Alberta, Canada

"There are many who are living far below their possibilities because they are continually handing over their individualities to others. Do you want to be a power in the world? Then be yourself. Be true to the highest within your soul and then allow yourself to be governed by no customs or conventionalities or arbitrary man-made rules that are not founded on principle."

— RALPH WALDO TRINE
1866-1858

What have we been programmed with (that we may have never even considered) that might be creating a barrier to our evolution? Many fear-based ideas — ideas that promote the notion of 'us' versus 'them,' thereby producing separation rather than unity. Some of those ideas are:

    ❀   "life is a struggle"

    ❀   "you must fight for your fair share because there isn't enough"

❖   "fear others"

❖   "keep your distance from anything dangerous"

❖   "be cautious, suspicious, wary, skeptical"

❖   "beware of ulterior motives"

❖   "blame, scream, shout, and lament about the miseries of life and injustices you observe or experience"

❖   "you are a helpless victim of forces beyond your control"

❖   "everything in life is either luck, an accident, or circumstantial"

We were *not* programmed to look for points of harmony or to simply love. *Why?* Because we're playing the 'Game of Life' without a full deck. We don't yet comprehend the 'bigger picture' — how and why things happen. That knowledge, although privy to those in the highest memes, is not yet *universally* known and one of the most important reasons, I believe, the events of September 11 occurred.

The Buddha said:

> *"The cause of all pain and suffering is ignorance."*

The time has come for this information to become universally known, for *until* we are playing the 'Game of Life' with all of the cards, hatred, crime, illness, racism, famine, confusion, and all of the other ills that have long plagued humankind, will not only continue to dominate life on Earth, but grow in magnitude and intensity. And in the wake of September 11, we can now add to that list of torments: easily obtainable nuclear bombs that fit inside a suitcase, as well as biological weapons.

Unaware of the 'bigger picture,' we instinctively retreat to the safety and security of our comfort zones when we encounter aspects of life that are not aligned with our programming. The result? Our evolution is arrested and an imbalance in our being is created. To regain our equilibrium, we must first acknowledge that another truth, one we are now unaware of, exists. And, as Einstein stated, that truth dwells at the *next* level of consciousness, thereby catalyzing our evolution into that level.

We will only regurgitate the past unless we acknowledge that truth is an ever-evolving aspect of life. We must accept that what we believe today is subject to reassessment. In *Conversations with God-book one,* it is explained that we must question what we now deem as truth:

> *"[Y]ou don't want to know the Truth, you want to know the Truth as you understand it. This is the greatest barrier to your enlightenment. You*

think you already know the Truth! You think you already understand how it is. So you agree with everything you see or hear or read that falls into the paradigm of your understanding, and reject everything which does not. And this you call learning. This you call being open to the teachings. Alas, you can never be open to the teachings so long as you are closed to everything save your own Truth."

— NEALE DONALD WALSCH
Conversations with God - Book 1 - pg 195

Though you may be tiring of my constant reminders, I promise that some of your beliefs, those you now deem indisputable and sacred, will be challenged as we move forward. Your first reaction? Fight or flee — to recoil and 'throw the baby out with the bath water.' However, to fully comprehend the higher purpose of September 11, each of us must now reevaluate what we currently deem as truth.

The events of September 11 shocked us into a new awareness, one that implores us to ask: *Why did we need to be shocked?* To understand why an event of such magnitude occurred, let's explore the next piece of the 'puzzle of life': Warnings imparted by others.

Many notable people have tried to warn that a considerable danger existed that was threatening humankind. As of yet though, no one has paid attention to these warnings. In the wake of September 11 the question is: Will we *now* listen and act on their admonitions, or will we ignore these warnings once again and go back to 'business as usual.'

CHAPTER IV

September 11
A 9-1-1 Emergency Call
to Humankind?

"You have to raise consciousness before you change consciousness."

— NEALE DONALD WALSCH
Conversations with God - Book 3 - pg 293

"The only thing that can possibly save humanity is for God to rise up within the human soul in the midst of great catastrophe."

— LEWIS MUMFORD
The Pentagon of Power

Before examining the threat posed to humankind, it is necessary to have a basis of understanding. So, let's revisit the premise of Spiral Dynamics and take it a step further. Just as each of us, the microcosm, progresses through various stages of development in our personal evolution, the same is true of humanity, the macrocosm. Looking back through history, you can clearly see that humanity has progressed through distinct stages, from survival, to forming clans, to worshiping mythical gods, to having religion dictate most aspects of life, etc. As humankind gained more and more collective experience, we gained greater and greater consciousness, thus facilitating the move into higher and higher memes.

As we progress through the various stages of evolution, a dominant meme always holds the 'seat of power.' This meme is at the helm of humankind's evolution and reigns until dissonance sets in and we can see its pros and cons from an unbiased perspective, thereby signaling our readiness to move onto the next meme. Today, that reigning meme is science and technology. As a society, we are more influenced by science than we are any other meme. While religion also has a significant influence on humanity, its power has waned. Because it has already held the seat of power, it has been relegated to the back seat, as Spiral Dynamics says it must.

While that information may seem insignificant, you will soon discover that science and technology, also playing the 'Game of Life' without a full deck, are playing an extremely dangerous game. Why? In many areas of technology, the underlying *intent* of research and development is not the betterment of humanity, but 'protecting' a select few from seemingly dangerous others — the belief in survival based on a misguided perception of 'us versus them.' That erroneous fallacy lies at the genesis of the dire threat posed to humankind, because that underlying *intent* has unfathomable power; power that is capable of destroying the human race. (We'll cover this premise extensively in subsequent chapters). This is one of the reasons that Albert Einstein, among others, warned that we must *advance our thinking* if humankind is to survive.

Keep in mind though, smaller adverse incidents are 'wrong-way' signs, warnings that *precede* a larger crisis allowing us the opportunity to intervene. However, if we fail to heed these warnings, they can only beget catastrophe. In light of the preceding information, ask yourself *where we are* and *the direction we are now headed in* as you read the following admonitions.

> *"Humankind is standing precariously on the edge of its destiny. It will either rise to a paradigm change or experience decline and possible destruction. This is an unavoidable confrontation."*
>
> — GLENDA GREEN
> *Love Without End: Jesus Speaks - pg 140*

> *"I believe that human survival in the face of the threat of nuclear holocaust and the devastation of our natural environment will be possible only if we are able to radically change the methods and values underlying our science and technology."*
>
> — FRITJOF CAPRA
> *The Tao of Physics - pg 335*

"Your present technology is threatening to outstrip your ability to use it wisely. Your society is on the verge of becoming a product of your technology, rather than your technology being a product of your society. When a society becomes a product of its own technology, it destroys itself."

— NEALE DONALD WALSCH
Conversations with God - Book 3 - pg 276

"Concern for man and his fate always forms the chief interest of all technical endeavors. Never forget this in the midst of your diagrams and equations."

— ALBERT EINSTEIN
1879-1955

"We've arranged a global civilization in which most crucial elements profoundly depend on science and technology. We've also arranged things so that almost no one understands science or technology. We might get away with it for a while, but sooner or later, this combustible mixture of ignorance and power is going to blow up in our faces."

— CARL SAGAN
1934-1996

"One of humanity's constant nightmares has been that technological growth...has always run ahead of...growth in wisdom, care, and compassionate use of that technology. In other words, exterior development has run ahead of interior development."

—KEN WILBER
A Theory of Everything - pg 103

In the novel *One*, Richard Bach explored a hypothetical planet Earth thousands of years from today:

"Evolution made civilization steward of this planet. One hundred thousand years later, the steward stood before evolution not healer, but parasite... a gifted society in so many ways, trapped at last by its greed and lack of vision. It ravaged the forests into desert, consumed the soul of the land in mine-pits and waste, smothered its air and its oceans, sterilized the earth with radiation and poisons. A million million chances it had to change, but it would not. From the ground it dug luxury for a few, jobs for the rest, and graves for the children of all. In the end, the children didn't agree, but the children had come too late... How could a civilization have been so blind?"

— RICHARD BACH
One - pp 227–228

"We stand at a critical moment in Earth's history, a time when humanity must choose its future. As the world becomes increasingly interdependent and fragile, the future at once holds great peril and great promise. To move forward we must recognize that in the midst of a magnificent diversity of cultures and life forms, we are one human family and one Earth community with a common destiny."

— PREAMBLE TO THE EARTH CHARTER
www.earthcharter.org

"All our lauded technological progress — our very civilization — is like an axe in the hand of a pathological criminal."

— ALBERT EINSTEIN
1879-1955

"Before the seventeenth century, the goals of science were wisdom, understanding the natural order, and living in harmony with it. In the seventeenth century this attitude..changed into its opposite. Ever since [that time] the goal of science has been [the acquisition of] knowledge that can be used to dominate and control nature. Today both science and technology are used predominantly for purposes that are dangerous, harmful, and antiecological."

— FRITJOF CAPRA
The Tao of Physics - pg 335

In *Conversations with God*, we are told it is imperative that we take a hard look at the unleashed power of science and technology. For as technology advances without a fundamental understanding of how life operates, an ominous potential for mankind is created.

"By developing medicines to do the work that your bodies were intended to do, you've created viruses so resistant to attack that they stand poised to knock out your entire species...If you are not careful, your own technology — that which was created to serve you — will kill you."

— NEALE DONALD WALSCH
Conversations with God - Book 3 - pg 278

"Science is but a perversion of itself unless it has as its ultimate goal the betterment of humanity."
— NICOLA TESLA
1856-1943

It appears that we, as humankind, are now at a crossroads in our evolution where we must advance our thinking if we are to balance all aspects of our being — body, mind, and spirit — for if we do not, the consequence could be fatal. We must now ask ourselves: *"Where are we"* and *"Where are we going?"* Have we ever considered who is at the helm of our evolution, the caretaker of our planet? And more important, do they have the best interests of *humanity* in their hearts? This issue is about the world, friends — the human race. It reaches far beyond the United States.

Could the tragedies of September 11, as well as the additional crises we are now encountering, be forms of 'Divine Intervention' — 'wake-up' calls alerting us to look deeper and ask questions before something *even more drastic occurs?* Before raising an eyebrow or rolling your eyes, let's explore a few 'coincidences.'

DIVINE INTERVENTION???

"Mystical experience is no stranger than other phenomena in nature."
— KARL PRIBRAM
Brain Scientist

"The stories in 'Hot Chocolate for the Mystical Soul' are for those ...who know...that an unseen loving presence is watching over us. Author Joan Borysenko has said that 'America is a nation of closet mystics.'...This book is proof that many of us are having mystical experiences with increasing regularity. [Through these stories] you will discover that there is a rhyme and reason to the Universe, and that the events in our lives are not random."

— ARIELLE FORD
Hot Chocolate for the Mystical Soul - Introduction

Statistics reveal interesting data on train crashes: On a day that a crash occurs, up to 30 percent fewer people are traveling than normal. *Coincidence?*

After the 1995 bombing of the federal building in Oklahoma City, a number of stories emerged about people who received a 'sign,' or had an unusual circumstance dramatically intervene in their lives, that prevented them from going to the building that fateful day. *Coincidence?*

On September 11, the four doomed terrorist flights had more than one thousand seats available, yet only two hundred and sixty-six people were aboard. *Coincidence?*

The World Trade Center employs more than 50,000 people, yet only 25,000 were in the buildings when the first jet hit. *Coincidence?*

Many people employed at the World Trade Center explained to the media that they were late for work or had been delayed by traffic on that portentous day. *Coincidence?*

The World Trade Center towers didn't collapse upon impact which allowed approximately twenty-two thousand people the time to escape. *Coincidence?*

The World Trade Center towers didn't topple over either. They fell inward averting even further tragedy. *Coincidence?*

A church very close to the World Trade Center remained unscathed despite the fact that other buildings around it were destroyed. *Coincidence?*

As workers removed rubble from the fallen World Trade Center towers, they uncovered something amazing: two intersecting steel beams had shorn off perfectly to form a huge cross. *Coincidence,* or could this phenomenon have been symbolic of the higher purpose of this tragedy?

Are you beginning to appreciate the gravity of the current state of being in our world; the direction of the path we are now embarked upon? And though I don't want to get too 'cosmic,' could 'unseen forces' be trying to guide us?

Before getting ahead of ourselves though, allow me to present the remaining 'evidence,' for there's far more to this story than what I have conveyed so far.

Ancient prophecies from civilizations all over this globe indicate that the time we are now living was to be among the most pivotal periods in the history of humanity. During this specific interval of time, each of us on Earth would be given an unprecedented 'window of opportunity' for a momentous leap in our evolution.

> "It is important to understand that current planetary crisis is a transitional aspect of an immense evolutionary turning point. The cosmological context within which world prophecy unfolds provides a coherent framework for understanding world events and trends, and where they are leading."
>
> — MOIRA TIMMS
> *Beyond Prophecies and Predictions - pg 24*

> "For whatsoever things were written aforetime were written for our learning, that we, through patience and comfort of the scriptures, might have hope."
>
> — THE BIBLE
> *The Book of Romans 15:4*

Let's now examine the intriguing prophecies; additional pieces of the 'puzzle of life' that when connected with others, shine a new light on both the events of September 11, and life itself.

CHAPTER V

The Shift of the Ages

"There is a process of unprecedented change unfolding within the earth. You are a part of that change. Without knowledge of the artificial boundaries of religion, science, or ancient mystic traditions, the change is characterized as dramatic shifts in the physical parameters of Earth accompanied by a rapid transformation in human understanding, perception, and experience. This time is historically referred to as 'The Shift of the Ages'."

— GREGG BRADEN
Awakening to Zero Point: The Collective Initiation

"The Ancients knew something which we seem to have forgotten."

— ALBERT EINSTEIN
1879-1955

Ancient prophecies from all over our world have shared something in common for millennia. They agree that sometime around the year 2000 (the Mayans more specifically stating from 1992 to 2012), humanity would undergo a radical transformation in consciousness, a quantum leap, a paradigm shift of enormous magnitude. These documents of antiquity tell us that greater truths would be revealed that explained life from the most fundamental level; truths that would provide a greater understanding, comprehension, and clarity about certain quandaries that have long baffled humankind. This truth would be capable of verifying reality from every realm of life, for it would transcend physical reality and distill it into simple understandings.

> *"You shall know the Truth and the Truth shall set you free."*

….we were promised in the Bible.

This transformation of consciousness, referred to by some as the "Shift of the Ages" and to others as the "Great Awakening," was recorded in ancient documents left by the Egyptians, Hopi Indians, Mayans, Lakota Sioux Indians, Essenes, Tibetans, and the Hindus, as well as certain brotherhoods that have existed for centuries: the Rosicrucians, Free Masons, and Jewish Kabalists. The ancient teachings further indicate that *only* during this specific period of time would humankind have attained sufficient technological knowledge and life experience to be able to comprehend this Truth and utilize it with wisdom.

The ancient texts further indicate that many paths, or potentialities, exist for humankind to take. And then they add something titillating, for they allude that we, as humankind, must consciously *choose* our future path from this point forward in our evolution. So let's now briefly explore the specifics of some of these prophecies.

THE PROPHECIES OF THE ANCIENT MAYANS

The ancient Mayan civilization, the word Maya meaning *illusion*, spoke of the 'end of time' as we know it, referring to the measurement of time. Their calendar, which spans 18,000 years, ends in the year 2012. The shift was prophesied to occur from 1992–2012, indicating that we are currently in the middle of this shift. According to the Mayans, this period of time marks the end of the "Fifth Age of Man," the "Age of the Intellect," and begins the "Sixth Age of Man," the "Age of the Gods." During this period the illusion of pain and separation would end, allowing us a more comprehensive understanding of life.

THE PROPHECIES OF THE HOPI INDIANS

The Hopi Indians, 'Hopi' meaning "people of peace," believe that the human race has passed through three different worlds since the inception of life on Earth. Their prophecies state that we are now at the end of the "Fourth World of Destruction," and beginning the "Fifth World of Peace."

In an email forwarded to me from Chief Dan Evehema of the Hopi Sovereign Nation in Hoteville, Arizona, I learned even more about the Hopi prophecies. Chief Evehema explained that the Earth, and all living things, were placed in the hands of certain Hopi who were ordained into the highest religious orders. These Hopi took an oath vowing to be a parent to all life on earth, and obligating themselves to advise and correct the children of earth in whatever peaceful way they could.

The objective of Chief Evehema's message was to unveil the last warnings and instructions to humankind before the "Fifth World of Peace" commenced. He states that humankind now stands at a crossroads, a critical point of decision where we must *choose* either everlasting life or total destruction. We are advised to *"recognize the true path of the Great Spirit"* — a path where we see one another as brothers and sisters, for *"there is no more time for divisions between people."* The Hopi prophecies further indicate *"that people with 'good hearts' must now release their fears and fulfill Earth's destiny of peace."*

Furthermore, the means of fulfilling this destiny is through "prayer" (the Hopi definition and process unlike that of Christianity's), for the Hopi believe that a human being's spiritual power through prayer is so potent that it decides life on earth. Chief Evehema closed his message with:

> *"Think good thoughts of peace and togetherness. Peace for all life on Earth and peace with one another in our homes, families, and countries. We are not so different in the Creators eyes. The same great Father Sun shines his love on each of us daily just as Mother Earth prepares the sustenance for our table, do they not? We are one after all."*

Robert Boissiere, in *Meditations with the Hopi*, affirms that two paths exist for humankind to choose from. Like Chief Evehema, he states that a time would come when each of us would be called upon to choose one path or the other:

> *"If we hold fast to the sacred way as He [the Great Spirit] devised it for us, what we have gained, we will never lose. But still, we have to choose between the two ways. When earthquakes, floods, hailstorms, drought, and famine will be the life of every day, the time will have then come for the return to the true path."*

Boissiere then conveys something interesting in the wake of September 11, for he states that we would know that the time had come to choose our path when: *"the earth [had] shaken three times."* The Hopi Elders contend that the first two 'shakings' have already occurred:

"First the Great War, then the second when the swastika rose above the battlefields of Europe ending in the Rising Sun sinking in a sea of blood."

But the third shaking was yet to come, and its magnitude would

*"...depend on which path humankind walks: the greed, the comfort, and profit, or the path of love, strength, and balance."*_{pg 117}

Could the events of September 11 have represented the "third shaking?"

THE PROPHECIES OF THE LAKOTA SIOUX INDIANS

The prophecies of the Lakota Sioux American Indians also spoke of the "Shift." And their prophecy is very intriguing. Approximately three hundred years ago, the tribe was curious as to when this phenomenon would occur, so they collectively queried the "Great Spirit." The response? The shift would begin when a special white buffalo was born. The father of this buffalo would die within two days of the birth, and then something even more amazing would occur. The buffalo would change its color four times; each color representing one of the root races in our world.

And true to the Lakota Sioux prophecy, in 1997 a white buffalo, the Lakota named 'Miracle,' was born. On the day following her birth, her father died of an aneurism. Astonishingly, her color then changed from white to black, to red, to yellow, and then *back* to white once more — exactly as the prophecy indicated, confirming to the Lakota Sioux that the great shift was beginning.

THE HINDU PROPHECIES

The Hindu measure time in "Yugas," four distinct ever-repeating eras that humankind progresses through in its evolution, a kind of 'cosmic change of seasons.' The 'season' we are now immersed in is referred to as the "Kali Yuga," the *"Age of Ignorance,"* an era characterized by darkness, suffering, chaos, greed, lies, and violence.

Within the Kali Yuga though, is a seed of redemption. For when life becomes almost intolerable, problems amplified, and hypocrisy reaches its zenith, man will thirst for truth, which will usher in the "Satyr Yuga," the *"Golden Age of Truth and Knowledge"*: an era of virtue and wisdom where misery, hatred, and illness no longer exist. The final annihilation of the Kali Yuga was prophesied to occur at a precise moment in time: *"in the twinkling of an eye,"* and would be followed by a 'purification.' This change in era would also be accompanied by a number of geophysical changes: changes in weather patterns, increased solar flares, and magnetic north shifting a few degrees. And true to the Hindu prophecies, each of those events is now occurring!*

The Hindu prophecies also indicate that great sages embellished with divinity would be born in this new era. And if you have had the opportunity to see Mattie Stepanek, author of the incredible book *"Heartsongs,"* I think you'll agree that that prophecy is manifesting also! Despite being afflicted with muscular dystrophy and having all of his siblings succumb to this disease, this magical angelic eleven-year-old has transcended his 'limitations' and recognized his true purpose: To be a peacemaker.

THE PROPHECIES OF THE ANCIENT EGYPTIANS

Perhaps the most enduring enigma on our planet was left by the ancient Egyptians whose technology still baffles science. This advanced race left an abundance of information in the form of hieroglyphics, as well as documents known as the "Emerald Tablets." Of note are specific hieroglyphics carved onto the walls and columns of Egyptian temples that clearly depict images of tanks, airplanes, rockets, etc. — objects not 'discovered' until years later. The Egyptians also left a very accurate Zodiac calendar, said to span 40,000 years, that documents the procession of the equinoxes. This calendar indicates that today, in 2002, we are progressing from the "Piscean Age" to the "Aquarian Age." Interestingly, this calendar is said to end on September 17, 2001.

*See Gregg Braden's *Awakening to Zero Point: The Collective Initiation*

Another fascinating 'factoid' was disclosed by an individual who "channels" information (acts as a conduit for information from other realms or dimensions of existence). This communication stated that sometime before the turn of the millennia, documents would be found in the Great Sphinx that detailed the history of humankind for the past 50,000 years. Of course, current science indicates otherwise. However, in 1997, through the technology of ground radar imaging, scientists discovered two chambers within the Sphinx that were previously not known to exist. Unfortunately though, the Egyptian government has not yet disclosed any information about this remarkable discovery.

THE DEAD SEA SCROLLS

"Oh, the Ancient Truth! Ages upon ages it was found, and it bound together a Noble Brotherhood. The Ancient Truth! Hold fast to it!"

— JOHANN WOLFGANG VON GOETHE
1749-1832

The Dead Sea Scrolls, ancient texts unearthed in 1947 that are approximately 2,500 years old, contain the Library of the Essene Brotherhood — teachings that provided much material for the Bible. These extraordinary documents were discovered both in Egypt in the Qumrum caves located next to the Dead Sea, and in a tomb in Nag Hamadi, Egypt in 1945.

Documents having the same origin were also purported to be found in 1881 in an ancient Buddhist monastery in Tibet by Reverend Gideon Jasper Ouseley. Moreover, correlative texts were discovered in the Secret Archives of the Vatican, as well as in the Royal Library of the Habsburgs (now the property of the Austrian government), said to have been brought out of Asia in the thirteenth century by Nestorian priests fleeing the hordes of Genghis Khan.

Who were the Essenes? They were folks similar to our native American Indians, people who lived in harmony with the elements and cycles of the earth. The most well known Essene was Jesus, for he was schooled extensively in the Essene teachings. In the early 1920's, Edmond Bordeaux Szekely, through an endless stream of 'coincidences,' discovered the Essene manuscripts in the Vatican library and translated them from their original Aramaic and Hebrew to French. Prior to his death in 1979, Szekely corroborated these manuscripts with fragments found in the Dead Sea Scrolls and found them to be of the same origin. In the introduction to the *Gospel of the Essenes* he tells us:

> "*From the remote ages of antiquity a remarkable teaching has existed which is universal in its application and ageless in its wisdom. Fragments of it are found in Sumerian hieroglyphs and on tiles and stones dating back some eight to ten thousand years. Some of the symbols are from an earlier age preceding the cataclysm that ended the Pleistocene period [the great Flood]. Traces*

of the teaching have appeared in every country and religion. Its fundamental principles were taught in ancient Persia, Egypt, India, Tibet, China, Palestine, Greece and many other countries. But it has been transmitted in its most pure form by the Essenes, that mysterious brotherhood which lived during the last two or three centuries B.C. and the first era of the Christian era at the Dead Sea in Palestine and at Lake Mareotis in Egypt. In Palestine and Syria the members of the brotherhood were known as Essenes and in Egypt as Therapeutae, or healers. The teaching appears in the Zend Avesta of Zarathustra, who translated it into a way of life that was followed for thousands of years. It contains the fundamental concepts of Brahmanism, the Vedas, and the Upanishads; and the Yoga systems of India sprang from the same source. Buddha later gave forth essentially the same basic ideas and his sacred Bodhi Tree is correlated with the Essene Tree of Life. In Tibet the teaching once more found expression in the Tibetan Wheel of Life. The Pythagoreans and Stoics in ancient Greece also followed the Essene principles and much of their way of life. The same teaching was an element of the Adonic culture of the Phoenicians, of the Alexandrian School of Philosophy in Egypt, and contributed greatly to many branches of Western culture, Freemasonry, Gnosticism, the Kabala, and Christianity. Jesus interpreted it in its most sublime and beautiful form in the seven Beatitudes of the Sermon on the Mount."

— EDMOND BORDEAUX SZEKELY
The Gospel of the Essenes - pp 127–129

The Essene teachings have had a long exciting history and appear to have permeated every nook and cranny of our world. Why did this Brotherhood conceal the knowledge they had acquired? As they observed the Roman Empire destroy anything in its path, they believed that the last remaining copies of what was to later become the Bible, would be destroyed. This compelled them to pen their knowledge onto papyrus scrolls and animal skins and secrete it for subsequent generations.

> "...and when the time came at last for the Brothers to leave the desert and go to another place, the scrolls stayed behind as buried sentinels, as forgotten guardians of eternal and living truth. A dark age began, a time of savagery, of barbarism, of book-burning, of superstition, and worship of empty idols. The gentle Jesus was lost in the image of a crucified god. The Essene brothers hid their teachings in the minds of a few who could preserve them for their descendants, and the scrolls of healing lay neglected beneath the shifting shadows of the desert..."
>
> — EDMOND BORDEAUX SZEKELY
> *The Discovery of the Essene Gospel of Peace - pg 14*

Found as thousands of fragments, the Dead Sea Scrolls were initially seen by few as they were painstakingly pieced back together. But in 1991, they were finally released to the public. Discovered in 1947, relatively recently, their translations are said to be far more accurate than previous ancient documents for they have been subjected to less interpretation and editing. Upon close examination, however, the Essene texts were found to differ from our modern Bible (i.e., the old and new testaments and the Sacred Books of the Avestas) — 70% were different, 20%, similar, and 10%, identical. The discrepancies within the texts can be accredited to the decisions and judgements made by the Council of Nicea, appointed by Constantine, the Roman Emperor in 325 A.D., for it was he who determined which texts would be included or omitted in the book that was to become the Bible.

This council of scholars had a daunting task, for not only were many of the texts mystical in nature, redundant, or simply not understood by the people of that time, but the scholars also had to make sure that Constantine would approve of the texts and convert to Christianity. As you may be aware, Christianity was not very popular with many Romans, as graphically depicted in the movie "*Gladiator*" where Christians were frequently sacrificed in the barbaric gladiator games. Constantine had opposed the Christian teachings because they required that one abstain from eating the flesh of animals and drinking alcoholic beverages, both of which most Romans had come to enjoy immensely. Therefore, the scholars of Nicea feared that Constantine would not accept a religion which prohibited these 'pleasures,' and omitted or "corrected" the passages they knew to be 'deal breakers' from the texts. Their primary objective was noble and virtuous: to preserve Christianity for the two thousand years of darkness prophesied to follow the death of Jesus. It had also been prophesied that hidden documents disclosing not only the original intent of the ancient truth, but much more, were to be revealed at the close of those two thousand years (today), ensuring that humankind would finally become aware of this knowledge.

The *Essene Gospel of Peace - book 4,* contains an excerpt very similar to the Hopi teachings and prophecies:

> *"There will come a day when the Son of Man will turn his face from his Earthly Mother and betray her, even denying his Mother and his birthright. Then shall he sell her into slavery, and her flesh shall be ravaged, her blood polluted, and her breath smothered; he will bring the fire of death into all parts of her kingdom, and his hunger will devour all her gifts and leave in their place only a desert. All these things he will do out of ignorance of the Law, and as a man dying slowly cannot smell his own stench, so will the Son of Man be blind to the truth: that as he plunders and ravages and destroys his Earthly Mother, so does he plunder, and ravage, and destroy himself."*
>
> — THE ESSENE GOSPEL OF PEACE - BOOK 4
> *The Teachings of the Elect - pp 36–37*

One of the most interesting texts discovered within the Essene Library was the *Essene Book of Revelation*, for it too implies that we must now *choose* our future. Since the word 'revelation' is oftentimes associated with doom and gloom, let's examine the true meaning of this word. The dictionary defines 'revelation' as *"something revealed or disclosed; a striking disclosure of something not before realized."* With that definition in mind, let's take a look at the *Essene Book of Revelation* — the *'aha'* moments that John the Apostle experienced when he was taken to see the "one on the throne" by Angel guides. Like Ebenezer Scrooge, from this place John had a higher, more expansive perspective of life. In addition, he was instructed to *"write the things which thou hast seen"* for future generations.

John was first shown a book that was secured by seven seals — a book written expressly for humankind *"who art the lowest of low and the highest of high."* This book revealed the *"mystery of mysteries"* — a mystery having the power to bestow

> *"all glory, and wisdom, and strength, and power forever and ever to him who shall reveal the mystery of mysteries."*

As John opened this book he was amazed, for it did not communicate in words, but in images like a movie. In the first scene, John saw the incredible wealth given to man — the gifts of air, water, Earth, joy, life, creation, and the sun. But the next scenes were troubling, for they revealed that over the course of time man had abused these wonderful gifts, and then turned his back in disbelief when the "truth" was imparted to him. Man chose *not* to believe the *"secret of eternity"* — the message given by the Angel of the Earthly Mother. Incredulous at this response, John implored the angels:

> "Tell me the message. For I would eat of the Tree
> of life that grows in the Sea of Eternity."

But the angels knew that this secret could only be utilized from a state of higher consciousness and accountability. Mankind first had to see the err of its ways, and then make some changes before the *"secret of eternity"* could be conveyed, for it had to be lived consciously. John then observed what would occur if mankind did *not* become conscious — scenes that depicted the annihilation of mankind and Earth; scenes of horror, tragedy, and immense suffering.

After viewing these terrifying scenes, the Angel of the Earthly Mother asked John:

> "O Man, wouldst thou have this vision come to
> pass?"

John replied:

> "I would do anything that these terrible things
> might not come to pass."

The angel then said:

> "Man has created these powers of destruction. He
> has wrought them from his own mind. He has
> turned his face away from the Angels of the
> Heavenly Father and the Earthly Mother and he
> has fashioned his own destruction."

John replied:

"*Then there is no hope, bright angel?*"

And the angel said:

"*There is always hope, O thou for whom Heaven and earth were created.*"

John was then told that a time would come when

"*the mystery of God should be revealed to those who have eaten of the tree of Life.*"

He was then instructed to open the book once again.

"*And I opened the book, and I read therein what had always been, what was now, and what would come to pass. I saw the holocaust which would engulf the entire earth, and the great destruction which would drown all her people in oceans of blood. Then my vision changed, and I saw a new heaven and a new earth; for the first heaven and the first earth were passed away...And there shall be no more death, neither sorrow, nor crying, neither shall there be any more pain; for the former things are passed away. And I saw too the eternity of man and the endless forgiveness of the Almighty. The souls of men were as blank pages in the book, always ready for a new song to be there inscribed...*"

When John asked how the vision of "*Heaven on Earth*" could come to pass, he was told:

> *"Heed Thou, O man! Thou mayest step on the right path... and through thy being may course the golden stream of the Law... Behold I make all things new... I will give unto him that is athirst of the fountain of the water of life freely. He that overcometh shall inherit all things... Come ye, and let us walk in the light of the Law."*

After the 'Holy Law,' the 'mystery of mysteries,' referred to as *"the never ending abundance of the Tree of Life,"* was revealed to John (as it will be to you) he ended the account of his experience with:

> *"I have heard thy wondrous secret. Through thy mystic insight thou has caused a spring of knowledge to well up within me, a fountain of power, pouring for living waters; a flood of love and of all-embracing wisdom like the splendor of Eternal Light."* pp 87–106

❧

The ancient Essene documents, along with prophecies from other ancient cultures, appear to have a common thread running through them — a thread indicating that we, as humankind, must now *choose* our future path.

Let's now take a look at *further* evidence suggesting that we have arrived at a point in our collective evolution where we must *consciously* choose our future. This evidence is found in a twentieth century enigma: The highly controversial Bible Code.

 CHAPTER VI

The Bible Code

"But thou, O Daniel, shut up the words and seal the book until the time of the End."

— THE BIBLE
Daniel 12:4

"The rule is that all that was, is, and will be unto the end of time is included in the Torah, from the first word to the last word. And not merely in a general sense, but as to the details of every species and each one individually, and details of details of everything that happened to him from the day of his birth until his end."

— THE GENIUS OF VILNA
an 18th Century Sage *The Jewish Mind - pp 33–34*

Though seemingly preposterous from our logical rational perspective, the original five Hebrew books of the Bible, known as the Torah, appear to contain a code within their text which reveals current, future, and past events — information clearly unavailable to humankind 3,200 years ago when the words were first imparted to Moses. Considered by some to be perhaps the most compelling enigma in history, clusters of words appearing in crossword-puzzle fashion, have disclosed 20th century events, such as the Kennedy assassinations, the Rabin assassination, World Wars I and II, the Shoemaker-Levy comet striking Jupiter, the Gulf War, and yes, the September 11 tragedies. Given the query *"Bin Laden,"* the words, *"Bin Laden, His Hand; Know that the Heart of Bin Laden is Snow,* and others appear in the Bible Code. (see www.biblecodedigest.com). Clearly, these events could not have been foreseen in the *past*, that is, if the past is truly 'past.'

> *"The distinction between past, present, and future is only an illusion, however persistent. Time is not at all what it seems. It does not flow only in one direction, and the future exists simultaneously with the past."*
> — ALBERT EINSTEIN
> *1879-1955*

Rather than delving into a fascinating topic that would distract us from the matter at hand, let's continue our exploration of the Bible Code. What the heck is this Bible Code, where did it come from, and how does it work?

The Bible code dates back to medieval times when rabbinical scholars first wrote about the discovery of meaningful words hidden in the Hebrew text of the Torah. They stated that everything and everyone that was, or will be, is recorded in these books. Furthermore, caution was given to scholars not to alter the words, for even one letter lost or altered from the original words could bring about the end of the world!

Okay.... Now to most, that kind of conjecture sounds pretty farfetched. The world destroyed because of a missing letter...? In spite of these dubious claims, many distinguished scholars have attempted to break the Bible Code. Among the more elite was Sir Isaac Newton, the father of Newtonian Physics, who was said to have become 'addicted' to breaking the code. After retiring his post at Cambridge University in 1696, Newton left a multitude of papers at the university that were discovered years later by John Maynard Keynes, his biographer. Much to Keyne's amazement, the volumes of hand written notes did not make reference to mathematics or astronomy, the subjects' Newton had become famous for, but instead esoteric theologies. It was quite apparent that Newton believed that the Bible contained a hidden prophecy of human history. In fact, he was certain that the Bible was a "cryptogram set by the Almighty" and wanted very much to "read the riddle of the Godhead, the riddle of past and future events divinely foreordained."*

*From "Essays and Sketches in Biography" Meridian Books, 1956 pp 280–290

Unfortunately, Newton was unable to crack the code, but another scholar, more than 200 years later, was able to uncover a key element of the code which eventually allowed others to break it.

That scholar was Rabbi Michael Ber Weissmandl, a Slovakian rabbi, who is considered to be the father of the Bible Code. Through tenacity and perseverance, the Rabbi discovered the basis for unraveling the code — an equidistant letter sequence, referred to as an "ELS." Simply, if you begin with the letter "T" (tav in Hebrew) in the book of Genesis and skip fifty letters, you will find the letter "O." If you skip another fifty letters, you will find an "R," and so on, using the same letter skip of fifty until you spell out the word "Torah" in Hebrew. This specific ELS code appears not only in the book of Genesis, but also the books of Exodus, Numbers, and Deuteronomy. In each of these instances, the letter skip sequence, the ELS, is identical. In subsequent searches it was found that the number of letters between meaningful words differs. And today, scholars believe that a significant correlation exists between a lower numerical letter skip and higher probability of occurrence.

How did the Bible Code move from obscurity to the international spotlight? The story began with the German "Enigma Code" which was developed in World War II. Through the laborious efforts of the Allies to break this complex code, many statistics, probabilities, and data were compiled, which gave birth to the invention of the computer.

As the computer evolved and became faster and faster, interest in breaking the code was revitalized, until finally, in 1994, two scientists succeeded in unraveling this mystery! Former physics graduate student, Doron Witzbum, and world-renowned mathematician, Eliyahu Rips, with the assistance of computer expert Yoav Rosenberg, stunned the world with their discovery of the code, first published in the journal *"Statistical Science."*

Prior to publishing these astonishing results, the findings of Rips and Witzbum were subjected to intense scrutiny. *Statistical Science* appointed a panel of referees to review and verify them, but after taking years to complete this process, the referees found that the math used to ascertain the findings was ironclad. In fact, it exceeded the criteria typically used as a benchmark. Editor Robert Kass wrote:

> *"Our referees were baffled. Their prior beliefs made them think the Book of Genesis could not possibly contain meaningful references to modern day individuals, yet when the authors carried out additional analyses and checks, the effects persisted. The paper is thus offered to 'Statistical Science' readers as a challenging puzzle."*

How did Rips and Witzbum crack the code? They simply eliminated the spaces and punctuation between words, essentially turning the original Torah into one long strand of letters — a clue intimated in folklore.

Controversy quickly erupted when the findings of Rips and Witzbum were published. Both the scientific and the religious communities vehemently challenged the results. But the topic was so hot, the information so incredible, it soon exploded on the world front. By 1997, a number of books disclosing this perplexing information became overnight sensations — among them *"The Bible Code"* by Michael Drosnin and *"Cracking the Bible Code"* by Jeffery Satinover.

> *"A great part of mankind now assumes that the Bible is just old folklore, myth, that science is the only reliable picture of reality. Others say that the Bible, the word of God, must be true, and therefore science must be in error. I think that, finally, when we understand both well enough, religion and science will come together — we will have a Unified Field Theory."*
>
> — ELIYAHU RIPS

Not only did the referees with *"Statistical Science"* find the code to be infallible, it was also proven valid by a number of other credible scientific sources. Famous mathematicians, the highest level Pentagon code-breakers, as well as esteemed professors at Harvard, Yale, and Hebrew University all agree that, although incomprehensible from our current knowledge base, the Bible Code is valid. This startling conclusion opened a big can of worms, for as you ponder the implications of the Code, the question arises: "Are we merely robots going through life with our destinies predetermined?"

The Bible Code says no, and here's where this information becomes relevant to the higher purpose of September 11. The Bible Code appears to present various *potentialities* that exist concurrently — a premise more fully understood with the advent of Quantum Physics, because it says the same thing. After a cataclysmic potentiality is spelled out, a haunting question then follows: "Will you change it?"

For example, after a scenario depicting "Heaven on Earth" is conveyed, it is followed by a scenario of doom and horror before the "End of Days." But following those two opposing excerpts, polar opposites of the same topic, the question is posed: "Will you change it?" In another example, after the phrase "Atomic Holocaust in the MidEast" appears (slated to occur in the near future…), the phrase "Will you change it?" follows. Will we? The question remains unanswered.

In his closing remarks in *The Bible Code*, author Michael Drosnin explains:

> "…the Bible Code is more than a warning. It may be the information we need to prevent the predicted disaster. 'Code will save' appears right above 'atomic holocaust,' just below 'the End of Days.' It is not a promise of divine salvation. It is not a threat of inevitable doom. It is just information. The message of the Bible Code is that we can save ourselves. In the end, what we do determines the outcome." pg 179

The Bible Code appears to provide yet further validation that we, as humankind, must now *choose* the future we desire.

This premise was also found in documents, alleged to be 36,000 years old, that were discovered in the Great Pyramid of Giza. They are known as *The Emerald Tablets of Thoth*:

> *"Know ye, O Man, that all of the future is an open book to him who can read. All effect shall bring forth its causes as all effects are from the first cause. Know ye that the future is not fixed or stable but varies as cause brings forth an effect. Look in the cause then thou shalt bring into being and surely thou shalt see all is effect."*
> — THE EMERALD TABLETS OF THOTH - TABLET 12

OVERCOMING OUR RATIONAL SKEPTICAL MIND-SET

Despite incontrovertible evidence, there are many skeptics who deny the Bible Codes' authenticity. But that's not unusual. Throughout history there have always been those who would not acknowledge the obvious — that the "emperor has no clothes on." Why do these folks refuse to acknowledge what is conspicuous to others? They would be forced to reevaluate their current beliefs — a scary undertaking, but again, a necessary undertaking if evolution is to occur. Resistance, it seems, always precedes momentous discoveries.

"If there is anything [that] human history demonstrates, it is the extreme slowness with which the academic and critical mind acknowledges facts to exist [that] present themselves as wild facts, with no stall or pigeonhole, or as facts [that] threaten to break up the accepted system."

— WILLIAM JAMES
1910-1942

"Throughout history, humankind has been resistant to change and to the acceptance of new ideas. Historical lore is replete with examples. When Galileo discovered the moons of Jupiter, the astronomers of that time refused to accept or even look at these satellites because the existence of these moons conflicted with their accepted beliefs. So it is now with psychiatrists and other therapists, who refuse to examine and evaluate the considerable evidence being gathered about survival after bodily death and about past-life memories. Their eyes stay tightly shut."

— DR. BRIAN WEISS
Many Lives, Many Masters - pg 10

"The attainment of wisdom is slow and painful, and few are willing to relinquish familiar, even if inaccurate, views. Resistence to change or growth is considerable."

— DR. DAVID HAWKINS
Power Versus Force - pg 195

Are you beginning to consider that there just might be a deeper meaning underlying the tragedies of September 11? Can you acknowledge that aspects of life exist that are now not a part of our everyday lives — that some of this "spiritual woo-woo stuff" may just be authentic? In case you're still on the fence, teetering between "No Way" and "Oh My God," I will present further validation that suggests that we indeed possess the ability to choose our future reality.

Let's now explore another significant piece of the 'puzzle of life' that provides solid scientific evidence, evidence that satisfies your left-brain's need for logic — Quantum Physics.

Living in a culture with a left-brain bias, science, the reigning meme that now holds the seat of power and thus has the greatest influence on our collective con-sciousness, provides us a 'respectable' credible resource for establishing viability to a topic that may be appearing a bit 'cosmic.'

CHAPTER VII

Quantum Physics

"*May the Universe in some strange sense be 'brought into being by the participation of those who participate?.... The vital act is the act of participation. 'Participator' is the incontrovertible new concept given by quantum mechanics. It strikes down the term 'observer' of classical theory — the man who stands safely behind the thick glass wall and watches what's going on without taking part. It can't be done, quantum mechanics says.*"

— JOHN WHEELER

Physicist - Princeton University - 'Gravitation' - pg 1273

> *"There are three paths leading to Truth. The first is the path of the consciousness, the second that of nature, and the third is the accumulated experience of past generations... From time immemorial, man and humanity have followed all three paths."*
>
> — EDMOND BORDEAUX SZEKELY
> *The Gospel of the Essenes - pg 13*

The destination of all paths is truth, for in applying that truth, we will ultimately live happier and more enjoyable lives. The path that I followed to discover truth was through experience, a right-brain approach, as opposed to the left-brain approach of nature or science. And though no one path is better than another, one may allow you to arrive at your destination more rapidly. Having arrived at the destination (humbly, I say tongue-in-cheek as truth is an ever-evolving aspect of life, and there is, in reality, no 'destination,' for the moment you discover one truth, you find that there are many many more...), I then wrote a book about how to apply this truth to everyday life. However, because the world-at-large has a left-brain bias, the truth derived from the path of experience is essentially 'unprovable' in a scientific sense, and as such, considered as 'nonsense' by many left-brain folks. ('Non-sense' = information that doesn't make sense or fit into an individual's belief system). Consequently, I knew that if the consciousness of humankind was to shift, science was key. Because science currently occupies the seat of power as the dominant collective meme and therefore has the greatest influence on humanity, science was necessary to render this truth, "Truth." So, I began my investigation into science to see how far it had come in its path to truth, and much to my delight, found that the science of Quantum Physics was on the cusp of determining that it is consciousness that creates life experience.

The path I followed to obtain truth also enabled me to see where science is getting 'hung up' in applying that truth to everyday life experience. And the largest obstacle I noticed is that science tries to fit new knowledge into old theories which unfortunately doesn't work. Therefore, the objective of this chapter is twofold: To disclose current scientific discoveries that suggest that we indeed have the ability to choose our future reality, and to illuminate the incongruities in science that are preventing it (and thus humankind) from moving forward in its evolution. This disclosure is essential, for it is only when we remove the obstacles from our collective path that we can evolve.

In this chapter, I will attempt to distill a few of the major principles in Quantum Physics, those funda-mental to my primary intent in this book — that consciousness, or thought, creates reality, and that we indeed possess the ability to choose our future. The principles I have included in this chapter do not begin to touch the surface of Quantum Physics. There are many important principles I have omitted: Niels Bohrs' "Principle of Complementarity," Schrö-dingers' "Wave Equation," and Max Born's "Proba-bility Interpretation of the Wave Function." I excluded them because I felt the presentation of too many principles would distract from my overall goal.

So please understand, this chapter is a very simplistic overview of Quantum Physics that may evoke more questions than answers. If you wish to dig deeper into this exciting science, but at the same time prefer to dispense with its mathematical equations, I highly recommend Gary Zukav's great work, *The Dancing Wu Li Masters: An Overview of the New Physics*. Gary masterfully renders a complex subject both comprehensible and exciting to those of us who are scientifically-challenged as he takes us through a journey of discoveries that one day will help to redefine life as we know it.

WHAT EXACTLY IS QUANTUM PHYSICS?

Although the words 'Quantum Physics' may sound formidable and perhaps even evoke a shudder in some, in reality, the basics of this science are not difficult to understand.

> *"Most of the fundamental ideas of science are essentially simple, and may, as a rule, be expressed in a language comprehensible to everyone."*
>
> — ALBERT EINSTEIN
> *1879-1955*

The science of Quantum Physics, also known as Quantum Mechanics, allows us to understand how life operates at the most fundamental levels of existence. It is the study of the physical nature of reality at the subatomic level of life — the level underlying our physical world. What does it say?

Rather than atoms being the basic 'building blocks' of physical matter (you, me, and everything else), as we were taught in school, at the subatomic level of life, those atoms are part of an invisible universe which is composed of patterns of energy — waves and particles that project various frequencies. The world at the subatomic level is a continual dance of mass changing to energy and energy changing to mass. (The E=M [energy=mass or matter] portion of the equation $E=MC^2$). Quantum Physics tells us that all matter projects specific wavelengths of energy — wavelengths so small they are unnoticeable. These energy frequencies are akin to radio, television, cellular phones, and microwave signals. Although we know they exist, they are not visible to our naked eye.

The frequencies of energy emanating from our bodies form an electromagnetic field of energy, a bioenergy field, often referred to as our 'aura.' And interestingly, this energy field is capable of being photographed using Kirilian photography, which was developed in the 1930's by Russian scientist, Dr. Kirlian. What appears on an aura photograph is most amazing for our energy fields project various colors. Every color in the color spectrum has a specific frequency of energy that corresponds with it. At one end of the spectrum are the low frequency colors beginning with red, and at the other, the high frequency colors of violet-white. On an aura photograph, the various colors represent the feelings, attitudes, or moods a person was, *in that exact moment,* projecting. This information is significant, for your electromagnetic bioenergy field reveals a lot about you and the life experiences you are creating.

NEWTONIAN PHYSICS VERSUS QUANTUM PHYSICS

How does Quantum Physics differ from classical Newtonian Physics? Newtonian Physics, named after Sir Isaac Newton (the Bible Code 'addict' — late 1600's), is based on the premise that our world operates independently of us through causal laws, such as the law of gravity. The law of gravity works whether we want it to or not, right? For all intents and purposes, gravity appears to be unaffected by our consciousness, and therefore it was assumed that *all* laws of nature were separate from 'us.' Hence, the conclusion was drawn that we are impotent bystanders in life subject to a myriad of unknown laws. Science surmised that if we were privy to these laws we could live in accordance with them and thus be more secure in our uncertain world. Sounds logical, doesn't it? So, the objective of Newtonian Physics was to determine these laws through observation and experimentation, essentially cause and effect, and then apply them in meaningful ways. Fundamental to classical physics is the assumption that we can observe life *impartially* — discover 'absolute' truths about nature and make future predictions based on that 'truth.' For example: "You have a high likelihood of developing cancer because your relatives did."

Based on those assumptions, science adopted rigid criteria for determining truth, stating that it could only be obtained through "empirical evidence": Results by one researcher must be capable of being duplicated and verified by other researchers using the same criteria. For example: if you and I apply the same criteria to a 'cause,' we will experience the same 'effect.' No aspect of reality could be considered as valid *unless* it passed the test of empirical evidence. If it couldn't pass the test, it was *suspect*, or even regarded by some as 'nonsense.' The only problem with that fundamental assumption? It was wrong.

> *"As scientists worked toward the elusive ultimate answers, bits of data here and there refused to fit into Newton's scheme. This is typical of any paradigm. Eventually, too many puzzling observations pile up outside the old framework of explanation and strain it. Usually at the point of crisis, someone has a great heretical idea. A powerful new insight explains the apparent contradictions. It introduces a new principle...a new perspective. By forcing a more compre-hensive theory, the crisis is not destructive but instructive."*
>
> — MARILYN FERGUSON
> *The Aquarian Conspiracy - pg 27*

Now, convincing science that one of its fundamental assumptions is inaccurate can be challenging. However, I will remind you once more that we do not have all the answers; that some of the 'laws' or truths we *assume* to be infallible, are in fact, quite fallible.

> *"A different theory…isn't that what has prefaced all major scientific breakthroughs and inventions throughout history? We discover a set of rules, formulae, or theories that apply and serve a purpose, and then discover that they must be modified or changed in order for us to progress further. It would seem that the laws of logic are inviolate, yet they can, on occasion, be eclipsed by others that supersede them. The higher principles govern the lower ones and foster the progression of human knowledge. One thing is certain, however: understanding the higher laws makes the lesser ones easier to deal with."*
>
> — MOIRA TIMMS
> *Beyond Prophecies and Predictions - pg 31*

"Take this new wonderful pill and you'll get better," is based on the current Newtonian definition of cause and effect which utilizes the methodology of empirical evidence. However, the inherent flaw in utilizing this approach to ascertain 'truth' was revealed time and again when 'proven' scientific truth — 'cause'— was found to have an 'effect' *only* in a percentage of cases. Rather than the 'new wonderful pill' having the *same* effect on all people as dictated by empirical evidence — "the test of truth" — when it came to *applying* that truth, the effects were mixed. Different people using the same 'proven cause' obtained different effects, for some people became well after taking the new wonderful pill while others didn't. And still others became well while taking a *placebo,* a sugar pill containing absolutely *no* medicinal properties.

> *"In 1950, Dr. Stewart Wolf studied women who endured persistent nausea and vomiting during pregnancy. These patients swallowed small, balloon-tipped tubes that, once positioned in their stomachs, allowed researchers to record the contractions associated with waves of nausea and vomiting. Then the women were given a drug they were told would cure the problem. In fact, they were given the opposite — syrup of ipecac — a substance that causes vomiting. Remarkably, the patient's nausea and vomiting ceased entirely and their stomach contractions, as measured through the balloons, returned to normal. Because they believed they received antinausea medicine, the women reversed the proven action of a powerful drug."*
> — DR. HERBERT BENSON
> *Timeless Healing: The Power and Biology of Belief - pg 33*

> *"[P]hysicians could no longer dismiss the phenomenon [of placebos] as a relatively minor factor, because now it seemed to have an effect the majority of the time."*
> — DR. HERBERT BENSON
> *Timeless Healing: The Power and Biology of Belief - pg 31*

The findings revealed by the 'placebo effect' were so blatant, they should have compelled science to question its basic assumptions — notably cause and effect. But that didn't happen. Rather than questioning the basis of this seemingly immutable law, science looked for another way out. Enter statistics and "margins of error." Now the line of reasoning went: *"Perhaps* you'll get better."

> *"If the facts don't fit the theory, change the facts."*
> — ALBERT EINSTEIN
> *1879-1955*

> *"We want the facts to fit the preconceptions. When they don't, it's easier to ignore the facts than to change the preconception."*
> —JESSAMYN WEST
> *1907-1984*

The reason that empirical evidence doesn't work? Cause and effect operates at the subatomic level of life, the quantum level. The future *cannot* be predicted, no 'wonderful pill' exists because Quantum Physics states that whether something is true or not, effective or not, is *subjective,* for it is only considered 'truth' when it corresponds with a person's experience. *Experience* is the name of the game — the beliefs and perceptions we hold as a result of those experiences. This is a fundamental premise that Dr. Herbert Benson, founder of the Harvard Mind/Body Clinic, uses to heal patients — some, incidentally, with 'incurable' illnesses.

> *"The only source of knowledge is experience."*
> — ALBERT EINSTEIN
> *1879-1955*

"Whether or not something is true is not a matter of how closely it corresponds to the absolute truth, but how consistent it is with our experience."

— GARY ZUKAV
The Dancing Wu Li Masters: An Overview of the New Physics - pg 38

"Perception... is a learned phenomenon. The world you live in, including the experience of your body, is completely dictated by how you learned to perceive it. If you change your perception, you change the experience of your body and your world."

— DR. DEEPAK CHOPRA
Ageless Body, Timeless Mind - pg 4

"The reality of the world lies in fields which interact with other fields of energy in dynamic chaos patterns that are always evolving to higher levels of complexity."

— DR. VALERIE HUNT
Infinite Mind: Science of the Human Vibrations of Consciousness - pg 49

Despite the fact that the premise of empirical evidence, cause and effect, has been called into serious question by Quantum Physics, science continues to apply that method of determining truth in almost every realm of research. Why? Science is caught in the middle, not quite sure how to apply the knowledge of Quantum Physics, but at the same time, fully aware that Newtonian physics cannot be adapted to the subatomic realm. To resolve this (hopefully temporary) dilemma, scientists decided they could have it both ways: Quantum Physics applies in the subatomic realm, and Newtonian Physics, in the physical realm. While that theory is valid in some areas, in others, it simply doesn't fly. Why? Quantum Physics was *proven* to work in all situations. Gary Zukav stated: *"This was one of the most important statements in the history of science."* Before delving deeper into this subject though, let's explore the origin of Quantum Physics.

THE GENESIS OF QUANTUM PHYSICS

In 1900, German physicist Max Planck (1858–1947) made one of the most important discoveries in the history of science, one he was not at all happy about for it questioned everything science held true about the nature of reality. What was this miraculous discovery that would undermine the foundation of Newtonian physics, the physics that shaped the world view for the previous two hundred years?

One of the last areas of research that eluded classical physics was the field of energy radiation. Essentially, science wanted to know how and why objects glow brighter as they become hotter, and change color when their temperature is either increased or decreased. Think in terms of a burner on an electric stove. When you turn it on, the element begins to heat slowly and smoothly, changing its color from black to red until you turn it off and it reverses that process. Newtonian physics assumed that all heated objects emit more high-frequency light than low-frequency, which implied that the burner should become white when heated rather than red. Consequently, scientists were perplexed when they found that heated objects *do not* radiate large amounts of high-frequency energy in the form of ultraviolet light, but instead radiate the low-energy frequency of red. Physicists referred to this quandary as the "Ultra-Violet Catastrophe," which inspired Planck to search for a resolution.

What Max discovered though, defied classical physics. For the findings he obtained while conducting his seemingly innocuous experiments indicated that energy was emitted *discontinuously*, in a series of incremental jumps *rather* than in a continuous flow. (Isn't that just the greatest discovery you have ever heard…?) And though my interpretation of this discovery is an ultra-condensed account of a monumental event, this seemingly trivial breakthrough opened the 'Pandoras Box' of Twentieth-century physics. For in the subatomic realm, the discontinuous release of energy happens to be the dominant characteristic of nature, making the nature of reality a whole new game.

Plank's findings ignited a chain reaction of other scientific discoveries, for just as the discovery of a few letters in a crossword puzzle sheds a new light on other words which before stymied you, the same is true of science.

*"The hypothesis of quanta has led to the idea
that there are changes in nature which do not
occur continuously, but in an explosive manner."*
— MAX PLANCK
"Neue Bahneneder Physikalishen," F. Albe, Phil Mag. Volume 28, 1914

All righty then.... To appreciate the impact of Planck's discovery on science and why Quantum Physics invalidates our current perception of cause and effect, let's explore a few of its offshoots.

BASIC TENETS OF QUANTUM PHYSICS
TENET #1: BELL'S THEORUM
MAN AND NATURE ARE ONE

John Bell, a physicist at the European Organization for Nuclear Research (CERN) in Switzerland created a mathematical construct which demonstrated that everything in the Universe is connected. Bell's Theorum provided the mathematical proof that man and nature are an interconnected part of an energy matrix composed of patterns of energy — a matrix that mystics would refer to as "Spirit."

*"All matter originates and exists only by virtue of
a force which brings the particles of an atom to
vibration and holds the most minute solar system
of the atom together.... We must assume behind
this force the existence of a conscious and
intelligent mind. This mind is the matrix of all
matter."*
— MAX PLANCK
1858–1947

Bell's Theorum provides us proof that life and the world around us are not as they appear nor as we have assumed. It demonstrates that we are not bystanders in life, but connected to everything and everyone by virtue of a matrix of energy. It presents rational proof that our rational ideas about the world are now outmoded. And though Bell's Theorum has been reformulated since 1964, its essence still maintains that everyday events do not occur as we thought they did, but in ways that are utterly different from what we currently believe.

"Bell's Theorum is the most profound discovery of science."

— HENRY STAPP

"The important thing about Bell's Theorum is that it puts the dilemma posed by quantum phenomena clearly into the realm of macroscopic phenomena... It shows that our ordinary ideas about the world are somehow profoundly deficient, even on the macroscopic level."

— HENRY P. STAPP
"S-Matrix Interpretation of Quantum Theory"' June 22, 1970

TENET #2 — HEISENBERG'S "UNCERTAINTY PRINCIPLE"

Let's move onto another principle that helps to explain why empirical evidence can no longer be used to establish 'truth' and why we must now remove this major hurdle on our path of evolution.

Fundamental to Quantum Physics is Werner Heisenberg's "Uncertainty Principle," a principle that demonstrates that we cannot observe nature, anything in the world, *without affecting it*. Gary Zukav explained this principle in the following manner:

> *"There are limits beyond which we cannot measure accurately at the same time, the processes of nature. These limits are not imposed by our measuring devices nor the small size of the entities we attempt to measure, but rather by the way that nature presents itself to us... As we penetrate deeper and deeper in the realm of the subatomic, we reach a certain point at which one part or another of our picture of nature becomes blurred, and there is no way to reclarify that part without blurring another part of the picture... [This is because] all attempts to observe the electron alter the electron...The whole idea of a causal Universe is undermined by the Uncertainty principle."*
>
> — GARY ZUKAV
> *The Dancing Wu Li Masters - pp 111–113*

> *"What we observe is not nature itself, but nature exposed to our method of questioning."*
>
> — WERNER HEISENBERG

To further illustrate the quandary posed by Quantum Physics and why it undermines the premise of empirical evidence, let's apply it to a real-life scenario. Assume you are a researcher wishing to conduct an experiment. *Why* do you want to conduct this experiment? You probably believe that it will provide you with information which will ultimately lead to the achievement of a goal. *Why* do you want to achieve this goal? Perhaps you want to resolve a problem that has long stymied humankind — to eradicate cancer or some other dreadful disease. *Why* do you wish to do that? Obviously, you would alleviate a great deal of pain that exists in our world. Sound reasonable? Now let's dig deeper. *Why* did you enter the field of research? What was your *intent* in choosing this particular profession? After all you could have chosen another vocation, one that put you on a Hawaiian beach where you escorted folks on excursions to swim with wild dolphins, right? But you chose the field of research, and you had a *reason* for doing so. And because you had a reason, you are biased.

Can you see how it is literally impossible to divorce yourself from your bias? To be an objective observer — again, a fundamental premise in Newtonian Physics — you must be *impartial,* have no opinion about what you are observing. However, as our example demonstrated, you cannot be unbiased. If you try to be objective, then your bias is to be objective, hence you have a bias, or opinion, right? The opinion that you can be without an opinion is an opinion. And Quantum Physics tells us that your bias or opinion will *influence* the results of your research; that, in fact, you cannot *not* affect the results of what you are studying by sheer virtue of your studying it. So rather than ascertaining unbiased 'truth,' the results of your research (and every other researcher), will reflect your (and their) bias!

> *"Physicists are now aware of subatomic particles that hover in and around everything that exists. One interesting characteristic of these particles is that they seem to take on the properties or expectations of the scientists studying them."*
> — LAURIE BETH JONES
> *The Path - pg 72*

THE PARADOX POSED BY QUANTUM PHYSICS

Science has indeed recognized the correlation between results and expectations, or bias, and sought to remedy this problem by conducting experiments using a "double-blind" approach. Simply, I give Suzy a list of ingredients and the instructions for a recipe without telling her what she's to make. She then passes the info onto Fred who cooks the 'mystery' dish. Fred is deemed the 'impartial observer' because he doesn't know what he is cooking, and the results of my recipe are supposedly distanced from my bias — my original 'great idea.' The only problem with that approach? It doesn't work. Quantum Physics suggests that you could, in fact, "million-blind" an experiment, and my intent, the wonderful dish I had originally envisioned in my mind, would *still* influence the results. Why? My consciousness and powerful intent are inseparable. Together they trigger a chain reaction within the matrix of energy, the interconnected whole of all existence — information conveyed and validated by numerous metaphysical sources, including the following:

"'The Cosmic Lattice' [A.K.A. 'The Matrix'] is a specific kind of energy, the energy of the Universe. It is the common denominator of the unified energy source. From the smallest particles of physics, to the electron haze forward, the Lattice is present. It has no visible light, even though it is the essence of light. When it is called upon and destabilized in designed ways, it provides power. It is the stabilizer of all energy and matter. The Lattice is in a constantly balanced state, and in that balanced energy it is potentially ready to receive input for the release of energy — input available to human consciousness. The Lattice 'sees' all time as zero, using naturally occurring physics for the mechanics of 'miracles'... The common physi-calness of the energy for power. It is one of the most powerful tools that exists today, and contains much of what you have called 'unex-plainable magic.' There is no greater power in the Universe than human intent and love! Do you understand that when you give intent, it is not some mysterious energy? Can you see that The Lattice has symmetry and size and purpose and consciousness, and that there is a mechanical attribute of physics and love around it called human intent?"

— LEE CARROLL
"The Cosmic Lattice," New Hampshire 1997 www.kryon.com

Psychic Powers, a volume from a series of Time-Life®
Books labeled *Mysteries of the Unknown*, explores a
theory, which when synthesized with information
from other realms, helps to explain why intent
cannot be separated from consciousness:

> "One of the most popular current metaphors for
> psychic communication relies on the paradoxical
> world view of quantum mechanics. This science
> describes matter at the subatomic level, where
> basic units are neither particles nor waves, but
> act like both, and where matter cannot even be
> said definitely to exist. Rather, it has a
> 'tendency to exist,' expressed as a mathematical
> probability. The micro world of subatomic
> behavior follows different rules from the macro
> world we know.... In a thought experiment — a
> famous example of this paradox — two particles
> — say, an electron, and its antimatter
> equivalent, a positron — collide, annihilating
> each other and creating two photons, which
> speed off in different directions. By the strange
> laws of quantum mechanics, photon A does not
> possess properties such as spin or velocity until it
> is noted by an observer; the very act of
> measurement is said to 'collapse its wave
> function' and assign it values at random. At the
> moment that observers do measure photon A,
> causing it to acquire a certain spin, photon B
> will acquire the opposite spin, no matter how far
> away it is. And despite having no connection
> with the first particle, Photon B somehow seems
> to 'know' instantaneously what photon A is

doing. This occurrence, confirmed in physical experiments, suggests that the Universe is connected in some hidden way, perhaps at a hypothetical sub-quantum level that includes our consciousness. If so, then clairvoyance, which supposedly enables a psychic to know instantly of an airplane crash miles away, may become plausible." pg 73

PROBABILITIES

"We do not know how to predict what will happen in a given circumstance. The only thing that can be predicted is the probability of different events."

— RICHARD FEYNMAN
Nobel Laureate Physicist

Quantum Physics is based on the idea of 'probabilities.' What does that mean? Rather than predicting future outcomes through cause and effect, as purported by Newtonian Physics, Quantum Physics states that only the 'probability' of something occurring can be predicted. Based on what I have learned from a synthesis of knowledge from a multitude of sources, I will take the premise of probabilities even further.

Think in terms of playing a game of Nintendo.® While playing this game you encounter moments where you must move your character, let's say, Mario, in one direction or another. Every time you must make a decision, you have arrived at a 'choice point' where a number of different directions or possibilities are available for you to choose from. With each decision, you activate a specific sequence of events — a 'ripple effect,' that determines which path you take and experience you have in this particular game of Nintendo.® From your higher perspective you can see the 'bigger picture,' for you recognize that embedded within this game are a number of predetermined, preprogrammed 'probabilities.' Each probability lies dormant awaiting activation until you make a choice. So, every time you reach a choice point and make a decision on Mario's behalf, you are actualizing one of those probabilities, as well as a specific sequence of events that will lead you in a specific direction.

Life is the same way. Quantum Physics provides the evidence that indicates that our realities, or life experiences, are based on the *choices* we make, consciously or unconsciously, each time we encounter a 'choice point' in life. Think about it. Throughout the day, at mind-boggling speeds, we encounter an incredible number of 'choice points,' from trivial to monumental. With each choice we make, we actualize a probability and sequence of events that follows. In other words, you are creating the experiences in your life based on the choices you are making, which also explains why a number of probable futures exist within the Bible Code.

Leading quantum physicist, Henry P. Stapp in *Mind, Matter, and Quantum Mechanics (1993),* states that reality is created by consciousness because consciousness, or bias (what an individual holds as knowledge), is the determining factor that actualizes a probability (causing the wave function to collapse) which, in turn, causes reality to "occur."

As in our game of Nintendo,® each of our choice points presents a number of potentialities. Today, as in times past, the majority of our choices, or probabilities, are actualized *unconsciously*, activated by our 'programming' — the contents of our comfort zone: our beliefs, thoughts, words, or actions. Each belief or bias we hold created a 'neural pathway' in our brain, a kind of 'downloaded' program which is automatically activated whenever we focus on a specific topic, thereby actualizing that specific probability and resulting life experience.

> *"The function of memory...is being studied by means of neural models among which attractor networks have been identified. Conclusions of current research are that the brain's neural networks act as a system of attractor patterns, and that stored memories act as attractors."*
> — DR. DAVID HAWKINS
> *Power Versus Force - pg 35*

The bottom line? We cannot eliminate ourselves from the "Game of Life." Whether we know it or not, accept it or not, or believe it or not, if we are alive and kicking, we are playing this game. The question is: Are we ready to begin playing *consciously?* The events of September 11 tell us that we must.

WHY HAVEN'T THE PRINCIPLES OF QUANTUM PHYSICS REACHED ALL THE SCIENCES?

"A truth once seen, even by a single mind, always ends up imposing itself on the totality of human consciousness. Evidence for this revolutionary thrust is issuing from all the sciences, and those who refuse to see it are blind. Evolution is a condition to which all theories must bow, a curve all lines must follow. No one can call himself modern who disregards this evolutionary thrust."
— PIERRE TEILHARD DE CHARDIN
1881-1955

"The more we mapped and named the physical phenomena in the universe, the more we could feel the world in which we lived was explained, predictable, secure, even ordinary and mundane. But in order to sustain this illusion we had to constantly screen and psychologically repress anything that reminded us of the mystery of life."
— JAMES REDFIELD and CAROL ADRIENNE
The Celestine Prophecy: An Experiential Guide - pg 24

"It is as if the same message keeps washing ashore, and no one breaks the bottles, much less the code... For all practical purposes, the West has only recently noticed the bottles that keep washing ashore and felt the tide that carriers them."
— MARILYN FERGUSON
The Aquarian Conspiracy - pg 82

The incredible discoveries made in Quantum Physics have yet to impact everyday life experience, perhaps because the implications require that we relinquish much of what we currently believe — something we are remiss to do on a *voluntary* basis. 'Change' is seen as a dirty word to most of us — something we dread. We like things to be the same. The status-quo provides security; it endows us a feeling of safety in what we currently perceive as an 'unsafe world.' So it is not accidental that the monumental discoveries made in Quantum Physics have not yet infiltrated everyday life, for Science has not yet agreed they are even valid, much less how to *apply* them.

> *"When new groups of phenomena compel changes in the pattern of thought... even the most eminent of physicists find immense difficulties. For the demand for change in the thought pattern may engender the feeling that the ground is about to be pulled from under one's feet...I believe that the difficulties at this point can hardly be overestimated. Once one has experienced the desperation with which clever men of science react to the demand for a change in the thought pattern, one can only be amazed that such revolutions in science have actually been possible at all."*
>
> — WERNER HEISENBERG
> *"Across The Frontiers," 1974 -pg 162*

> *"Why does this applied science, which saves work and makes life easier, bring us so little happiness? The simple answer runs: Because we have not yet learned to make sensible use of it."*
>
> — ALBERT EINSTEIN

Science has not learned how to apply this knowledge because Science doesn't hold the key. Science simply provides the *foundation* of understanding, it contributes *one* piece to the 'puzzle of life' that must be connected with others that *also* contribute important pieces.

"One believes that the conscious mind and the intellect have all the answers, but to this school …the conscious mind is analytical above all, and it can find all the answers through reason alone. The other school believes that the answers are in feelings and emotion. Both are wrong. Intellect and feeling <u>together</u> make up your existence, but the fallacy is particularly in the belief that the aware mind must be analytical above all, as opposed to, for example, the understanding or assimilation of intuitive psychic knowledge. Neither school understands the flexibility and the possibilities that are inherent within the conscious mind, and mankind has barely begun to use its potentials."

— JANE ROBERTS
The Nature of Personal Reality - A Seth Book - pg 171

"The intuitive mind is a sacred gift, and the rational mind is a faithful servant. We have created a society that honors the servant and has forgotten the gift."

— ALBERT EINSTEIN
1879-1955

"When the mind is reinforced by academic and intellectual pursuits, the heart will be over-shadowed."

— GLENDA GREEN
Love Without End: Jesus Speaks - pg 54

The discoveries made in Quantum Physics will be applied to everyday life experience when they are integrated with discoveries made in other realms, just as the study of life did in earlier days.

"The roots of physics, as of all western science, are to be found in the first period of Greek philosophy in the sixth century BC, in a culture where science, philosophy, and religion were not separated. The sages of the Milesian school of Ionia were not concerned with such distinctions. Their aim was to discover the essential nature, or real constitution, of things which they called 'physis.' The term 'physics' is derived from this Greek word and meant therefore, originally, 'the endeavor of seeing the essential nature of all things'."

— DR. FRITJOF CAPRA
The Tao of Physics - pg 20

When the knowledge of Quantum Physics is synthesized with that of other realms, when all the pieces of the 'puzzle of life' are connected, the "mystery of mysteries" will be comprehensive, allowing us, as humankind, to live from a point of power rather than victimhood.

"The influence of modern physics goes beyond technology. It extends to the realm of thought and culture where it has led to a deep revision in our conception of the universe and our relation to it. The exploration of the atomic and subatomic world in the twentieth century has revealed an unsuspected limitation of classical ideas, and has necessitated a radical revision of many of our basic concepts."

— DR. FRITJOF CAPRA
The Tao of Physics - pg 17

"As commonly used, [the term] 'paradigm' is intended to draw our attention in a somewhat coherent way to the fact that apparently unrelated social [or otherwise] phenomena are, in fact, significantly related. The concept encourages us to push beneath the surface to deeper levels of understanding at which the connections among apparently disparate data can be clearly seen and grasped."

— RUBEN NELSON
Reflections on Paradigms - 1993
a paper prepared for The Environmental Council of Alberta, Canada

"As in the case of the discovery of radio waves or x-rays, a sudden expansion of our awareness of the workings of the universe not only allows, but demands a recontextualization of our world view. Implications of new knowledge require a reworking of old ideas to form a larger context. Though it may occasion some intellectual stress, such scientific recontextualization of human behavior can expose the basic structures that underlie personal and social problems, thereby revealing their solutions."

— DR. DAVID HAWKINS
Power Versus Force - pg 10

As theoretical physicist, Dr. Fritjof Capra, explains in *"The Tao of Physics: An Exploration of the Parallels between Modern Physics and Eastern Mysticism:"*

> *"Modern physics leads us to a view of the world which is very similar to the views held by mystics of all ages and traditions."*pg 19

Regrettably, I don't have a great deal of faith that science will be able to shift its paradigm any time soon. My older brother is a biochemist, a research scientist, and firmly holds that empirical evidence must be garnered before anything can be regarded as valid. And though we have discussed the basic tenets of Quantum Physics that call into question the scientific definition of cause and effect, I have learned that any viewpoint that differs from the current scientific paradigm is most often categorized as 'nonsense.' Many scientists are not interested in hearing anything new, and will defend their (Newtonian) stance, however obsolete, like a mother who tenaciously protects her young.

> *"The important thing in science is not so much to obtain new facts as to discover new ways of thinking about them."*
> — SIR WILLIAM HENRY BRAGG
> *1862-1942*

There are some in the scientific realm, however, who *can* see past the current paradigm into the more expansive version of truth. For truth cannot be denied nor suppressed — eventually it will emerge, for truth is an ever-evolving aspect of life.

Despite enormous obstacles, a few daring souls are uncovering this knowledge and applying it with incredible results. These brave doctors have challenged the accepted dogma of the current paradigm. And though I am certain that hundreds exist, I would like to honor those I am aware of: Dr. Herbert Benson, Dr. Andrew Weil, Dr. John E. Sarno, Dr. Brian Weiss, Dr. Christine Northrup, and Dr. 'Patch' Adams, whose story was told in the movie *Patch Adams* starring Robin Williams. These visionaries have had the fortitude to not only brave the sneers of their colleagues, but also to jeopardize their careers in the name of a new Truth.

> *"A characteristic of a true artist or scientist is the firm confidence they have in themselves. This confidence is an expression of inner strength which allows them to speak out, secure in the knowledge that, appearances to the contrary, it is the world that is confused and not they. The first man to see an illusion by which men have flourished for centuries surely stands in a lonely place. In that moment of insight he, and he alone, sees the obvious which to the uninitiated [the rest of the world] yet appears as nonsense, or worse, madness, or heresy. This confidence is not the obstinacy of the fool, but the surety of him who knows what he knows, and knows also that he can convey it to others in a meaningful way."*
> — GARY ZUKAV
> *The Dancing Wu Li Masters: An Overview of the New Physics*

"Great spirits have always encountered violent opposition from mediocre minds."

— ALBERT EINSTEIN

"Again and again some people in the crowd wake up. They have no ground in the crowd, and they emerge according to much broader laws. They carry strange customs with them, and demand room for bold gestures. The future speaks ruthlessly through them."

— RAINER MARIA RILKE
1875-1926

Having taken a quantum leap into the dark abyss of controversy, the aforementioned courageous individuals, or 'Bringers of Light' (a higher frequency of light [photons] = higher knowledge, or truth), are helping to usher in a new stage of evolution for humankind: the time to see a 'new' truth and integrate it with the old, for that is what is truly needed now. Just as Rome was not built in a day, our trek across the bridge of consciousness will not be accomplished overnight. It will take time to transition into the application of our authentic power.

"Creating a new theory is not like destroying an old barn and erecting a skyscraper in its place. It is rather like climbing a mountain, gaining a new and wider view, discovering unexpected connections between our starting point and its rich environment. But the point from which we started out still exists and can be seen, although it appears smaller and forms a tiny part of our broad view gained by the mastery of the obstacles on our adventurous way up."

— ALBERT EINSTEIN

The miraculous 'pill' we were waiting for science to deliver, the panacea that would eliminate illness and make life better in a myriad of ways, is not forthcoming, for that 'pill' *exists within each of us* and always has. Despite the fact that we are unaware of our authentic power, we cannot escape the miracle of our being.

At the conclusion of *The Wizard of Oz* there is a scene where Dorothy believes that she will never be able to return to her loved ones back in Kansas. In that agonizing moment, Glinda, the good witch appears:

> *Dorothy: "Oh, Glinda, can you please help me get back to Kansas?"*
>
> *Glinda: "You don't need to be helped any longer. You always had the power to go back to Kansas. It was inside you."*
>
> *Scarecrow: "Why didn't you tell her?"*
>
> *Glinda: "She would not have believed me. She had to learn it for herself."*

Evolution, friends, is through experience. However, in our current state of consciousness, dominantly influenced by the beliefs of Newtonian Physics, people "won't believe it until they can see it." But

Quantum Physics tells us that the *opposite* is true, for whenever you encounter a 'choice point' in life, you can only manifest what you *believe* — your bias or opinion. So if you believe that you won't believe it until you see it, then *that's* the life experience you will actualize. However, if you wish to actualize a different probability, if you *really* want to see it, then you'll have to change your belief. To change a belief, which in essence, is nothing more than a *habit* of thoughts, you must leave your comfort zone. And seeing as the events of September 11 kicked you out of your comfort zone, it's a great time to build a new one — one based on a new level of awareness.

> "It's important now, it's time now, to change your mind about some things. This is what evolution is all about."
> — NEALE DONALD WALSCH
> *Conversations with God - Book 1 - pg 168*

> "We must acknowledge that we are in a magnificent era when the old is fading and the new has not been fully disclosed."
> — DR. VALERIE HUNT
> *Infinite Mind: Science of the Human Vibrations of Consciousness - pg 49*

We must now open our eyes to the incongruities in science. We must put the pieces of the 'puzzle of life' together and take responsibility for our own lives and the destiny of humanity. We can no longer place our faith in those who have a vested interest in maintaining the 'rules' as they stand today. The stakes are too high. People are dying every day because they have adopted the beliefs of science, thinking that no other options were available. We must acknowledge that Science, those to whom we have given our power, those at the helm of our evolution, will not be providing the avenue for the revolutionary, evolutionary leap in consciousness we now must take. Science has become so large, so complex, so deeply entrenched in its paradigm, that it is virtually incapable of 'moving on a dime' and reassessing its dogma any time in the near future. That is simply asking too much.

> *"If a scientist really examines the implications [of the Big Bang theory], he would be traumatized. As usual, when the mind is faced with trauma, it reacts by ignoring the implications — in science this is referred to as 'refusing to speculate' — or by trivializing the origin of the world [or any other subject that creates this trauma] by calling it the Big Bang, as if the Universe were merely a firecracker."*
> — ROBERT JASTROW
> *Head Astrophysicist at NASA's Goddard Institute for Space Studies*

> *"Science promised power.... but, as so often happens when people are seduced by promises of power, the price is servitude and impotence. Power is nothing if it is not the power to choose."*
> — JOSEPH WEIZANBAUM
> *Scientist, Massachusetts Institute of Technology*

The question posed to humanity boils down to which probability we will collectively choose for our future.

Will our solution to the September 11 attacks reflect our *current* level of awareness, actualizing the *"destruction, annihilation, oceans of blood"* probability, or will we have the insight, courage, and wisdom to actualize the *"Heaven on Earth," "peaceful world"* probability. It's our choice. And now, just as the ancient prophecies indicated, our future will be based on what we choose.

> *"Twentieth-century physics is the story of a journey from intellectual entrenchment to intellectual openness, despite the conservative 'prove-it-to-me' nature of individual physicists ... We are approaching the end of science. The 'end of science' does not mean the end of 'unresting endeavor and continually progressing development' of more and more comprehensive and useful theories. The 'end of science' means the coming of western civilization, in its own time and in its own way, into the higher dimensions of human experience."*
>
> — GARY ZUKAV
> The Dancing Wu Li Masters: An Overview of the New Physics - pp 312–313

> *"In its most recent stages, Western science is finally overcoming [a world view in sharp contrast to that of the Far East] and coming back to those of the early Greek and the Eastern philosophies. This time, however, it is not only based on intuition, but also on experiments of great precision and sophistication, and on a rigorous and consistent mathematical formalism."*
>
> — DR. FRITJOF CAPRA
> The Tao of Physics - pg 19

"Quantum science suggests the existence of many possible futures for each moment of our lives. Each future lies in a state of rest until it is awakened by choices made in the present."
— GREGG BRADEN
The Isaiah Effect - pg 7

How do we choose our future reality? How do we actualize the probability we prefer? What are the specific steps to take? Well, that just so happens to be the subject-matter of my book *"Life: A Complete Operating Manual."* In *"Life,"* I explain exactly how to harness the power of your thoughts to create what you want in life. However, since my objective in this book is to propose an effective solution to the September 11 tragedies, one that ensures a lasting peace, I will condense this explanation into something 'short and sweet.' If you would like the more expansive version, I recommend reading *"Life."*

The bottom line? It's time to expand our horizons and integrate the knowledge of Quantum Physics with that of other realms. For this integration will render the 'mystery of mysteries' comprehensible, which will in turn, usher in a new day for humankind. Before unveiling the mystery though, let's take one last look at where we are and where we are going at this precise moment in time.

CHAPTER VIII

Life Prior to September 11

"Our choice is between the painful, but confidence instilling process of coming to know who and where we are... and the immensely appealing but finally empty alternative of continuing to drift, of acting as if we know what we are doing when both the mounting evidence and our most honest fears indicate that we do not... In government, as in other relationships, we have the capacity to deceive ourselves, to shape the realities by which we live, so that our prime focus is on our comfort rather than the truth..."

— RUBEN NELSON
The Illusions of Urban Man
a paper prepared for The Canadian Government

"Most of us are passive because our awareness is constricted."

— MARILYN FERGUSON
The Aquarian Conspiracy - pg 193

"Why do we give away our power or never claim it at all? Perhaps so that we can avoid decisions and responsibility. We are seduced by pain-avoidance, conflict-avoidance."

— MARILYN FERGUSON
The Aquarian Conspiracy - pg 193

"The world is in the condition that it's in because the world is full of sleepwalkers."

— NEALE DONALD WALSCH
Conversations with God - Book 1 - pg 191

"With the poor and needy of the world already suffering beyond belief, catastrophe may be necessary to tear away the denials and delusions that insulate comfortable people and spoliational lifestyles. It certainly will induce a fertile psychic climate, one that traumatizes deeply enough to draw the liberating value of the hitherto dormant Self to the fore."

— MOIRA TIMMS
Beyond Prophecies and Predictions - pg 245

Now that you know a bit more about what was underlying the reason for a 9-1-1 emergency call to humankind, let's explore where we were and where we were going prior to that infamous day.

"On any journey, we must find out where we are before we can plan the first step."

— KATHY BOEVINK

Prior to September 11, most of us couldn't be bothered with world events. We didn't have time to look further and deeper, we had enough on our plates. We didn't want to be bothered with any more 'issues.' Bombarded with so many travesties on TV, we became overwhelmed and desensitized to them, primarily because we felt powerless to effect any kind of meaningful change. The result? We stopped thinking for ourselves and trusted others to think and act for us. We abdicated our power. And because our elected officials didn't want us to worry, to risk our fragile economy, or knew that 'unpleasant' information would probably not generate public support, many problems and issues never made it to the evening news. Consequently, we were unaware of how most of our national and international problems were being handled. After all, that's why we elected our officials, right? To do the 'dirty work' while we went about our day-to-day lives thinking of ourselves as a wonderful, caring, generous nation. Big mistake. However, it's not time to blame, it's time to awaken, because in truth, we're all at fault.

Perhaps you saw interviews where people stated that they *knew* a terrorist attack would occur. The evidence was blatant; it was just a matter of time…. In the aftermath of the September 11 tragedies, we have awakened to much we didn't know, much we cared not to know, and much we closed our eyes to. People hate us? Why? What have *we* done to deserve hatred? And now that our eyes are being opened, what steps can we take to end this hatred?

We have been deep asleep, oblivious to many events taking place all around us, unaware of the profound imbalance in our beings, incognizant that a serious danger was threatening humankind. But wait a second. Think about it. Would we have *seriously* considered warnings about the extinction of humankind? I don't think so. We'd find some excuse to label the messengers of that information as the 'lunatic fringe.' "The sky is falling, the sky is falling" would certainly be met with ridicule, suspicion, and jeers. So, what would it take to kick us out of our comfort zones; to jar us from our complacency? What would it take to overcome our deeply entrenched resistence?

Airplanes crashing into the World Trade Center Towers, the Pentagon, and the Pennsylvania country-side. Events so catastrophic, they would touch the whole of humanity. So, if this deplorable tragedy's higher purpose was to awaken us to dangers that we were unaware of, it's time we do something. This is not a dress rehearsal for life, friends, as evidenced by the deep pain, sorrow, and anguish that our country and the world experienced in the wake of September 11. As in the 1960's, we too, must open our eyes:

> *"I urge you to learn the harsh facts that lurk behind the mask of optical illusion with which we have concealed our true circumstances, even from ourselves. Our country is in danger. Not just from foreign enemies; but above all, from our own misguided policies, and what they can do to this country. There is a contest, not for the rule of America, but for the heart of America."*
> — ROBERT KENNEDY
> 1925-1968

Imagine that *you* were aware of a serious danger posed to an individual. What would you do? How far would you go? Michael Drosnin, a respected investigative journalist and author of *The Bible Code,* was put to the test when he discovered the authenticity of the Bible Code. He had found that the name 'Yitzhak Rabin' was encoded with the words *"assassin will assassinate."* Despite considerable risk to his reputation, career, and everything else he held sacred, Mr. Drosnin resolved to warn the Prime Minister of Israel *before* the event was to take place. Since he understood the nature of the Bible Code, he knew that this event was simply one potentiality out of many. Despite Drosnin's warnings, Rabin was skeptical, and on November 4, 1995 was assassinated — just as the Bible Code foretold.

If you were the pilot of an F-16 sent to shoot down a passenger airplane with hijackers, what would you do? Would you have the courage to gun down innocent people in order to save a greater number of lives? What did the heroes on flight 93, the flight that crashed into the Pennsylvania countryside do? Whatever was necessary to save a greater number of lives. Could that response be instinctive?

After a forest fire in Yellowstone National Park, forest rangers began their trek up a mountain to assess the inferno's damage. One ranger found a bird literally petrified in ashes, perched statuesquely on the ground at the base of a tree. Struck by this eerie sight, he gently knocked the bird over with a stick and to his amazement, three tiny chicks scurried from under their dead mother's wings. The loving mother, keenly aware of impending disaster, had carried her offspring to the base of the tree and gathered them under her wings, instinctively knowing that the toxic smoke would rise. Although she could have flown to safety, she had refused to abandon her babies. When the blaze arrived and scorched her small body, the mother remained steadfast. And because she had been willing to sacrifice her one life, the three babies huddled under the cover of her wings, lived.

— NATIONAL GEOGRAPHIC MAGAZINE
paraphrased

As we connect the pieces to the 'puzzle of life' and search for the higher purpose in these tragedies, is it possible that God's Master Plan included the deaths of three thousand forty-four souls so that six Billion could live?

"Then one of them, named Caiaphas, who was a high priest that year, spoke up, 'you know nothing at all! You do not realize that it is better for you that one man die for the people than that the whole nation perish.' He did not say this on his own, but as a high priest that year he prophesied that Jesus would die for the Jewish nation, and not only for that nation but also for the scattered children of God, <u>to bring them together and make them one</u>."

— THE BIBLE
John 11:49-52 (my emphasis)

Did three thousand forty-four people 'volunteer,' on a soul level, to jar us from our comfort zones so that we would unite and discover that an imbalance in our being was threatening the whole of humanity?

"Advanced technology without advanced <u>thought</u> creates not advancement, but demise."
— NEALE DONALD WALSCH
Conversations with God - Book 2 - pg 114

"We shall require a substantially new manner of <u>thinking</u> if mankind is to survive."
— ALBERT EINSTEIN
1879-1955

"It is important that we look beyond the immediate tumult of world events to the potential for resolution, rebalance, and healing. Inherent within the gestation period of prophecy is the tremendous power of intention and right action in averting it. Turmoil and confusion are integral parts of the equation today. Like leaking toxic waste, no longer containable below the threshold of awareness, today's chaos represents negativity, suppression, and denial becoming externalized into a conscious combustible force. If we do not deal with problems before they escalate, we deal with them when they combust!"
— MOIRA TIMMS
Beyond Prophecies and Predictions - pg 201

In order to evolve into the next level of consciousness, to choose our future reality, and resolve the crisis we now face, we must now advance our *thinking*. If three thousand forty-four souls perished to send us a message, we owe it to them to heed the 9-1-1 call they provided.

> *"For each circumstance is a gift, and in each experience is hidden a treasure."*
> — NEALE DONALD WALSCH
> *Conversations with God - Book 1 - pg 33*

> *"In the middle of every difficulty lies opportunity."*
> — ALBERT EINSTEIN
> *1879-1955*

The children of Earth have been given the "matches." A more expansive truth is being revealed exactly when it was prophesied — at a moment in history when humankind had attained capabilities that required conscious discernment and wisdom. For today we have developed technologies so advanced, we are capable of cloning our species, poisoning our ecosystems, irreparably damaging the critical balance of nature, and destroying our planet. Therefore, at this precise moment in time the questions posed to each of us are:

    ❋   How will we use these technologies?

    ❋   Have we learned from our past?

    ❋   Have we experienced enough anguish, enough suffering, enough hatred, enough separation?

❖ Have we reached our threshold of pain?

❖ Have we recognized the futility of war?

❖ Are we willing to look deeper and devise a solution to the quandary presented by September 11 at the next level of consciousness?

"The largest question facing the human race is not when will you learn, but when will you act on what you've already learned?"
— NEALE DONALD WALSCH
Conversations with God - Book 2 - pg 171

"Fatalism and indifference will never solve the monumental problem of how to avert world catastrophe. We must involve ourselves again with the miracle of life. We have opened the Pandora's box of nuclear energy; we can also open, with the key of truth, the hidden treasure house of ancient wisdom waiting to be discovered in a forgotten manuscript, an ancient scroll, or in the unknown seat of knowledge within ourselves. We must rediscover our place in the world-picture, our original role as the partner of the Creator, helping to sow and harvest and make the earth once more a Garden."
— EDMOND BORDEAUX SZEKELY
The Discovery of the Essene Gospel of Peace - pp 10–11

> *"Think of the earth as a living organism that is being attacked by billions of bacteria whose numbers double every forty years. Either the host dies, or the [parasite] dies, or both dies."*
> — GORE VIDAL

Perhaps our response to the tragedies of September 11 is a test for each of us individually, and all of us collectively — a test that will determine whether we graduate to the next level of consciousness or are doomed to repeat this lesson until we 'get' it.

> *"Those who do not learn from history, are doomed to repeat it."*

I wonder if wagers are being made somewhere in the cosmos....

> *"[T]he question is not: Why start off on a such a path? You have already started off. You did so with the first beat of your heart. The question is: Do I wish to walk this path consciously, or unconsciously? With awareness or lack of awareness? As the cause of my experience, or at the effect of it?"*
> — NEALE DONALD WALSCH
> *Conversations with God - Book 1 - pg 156*

All right, time for the drum roll. One of the most significant pieces of the 'puzzle of life' is about to be unveiled, the mystery of mysteries revealed: *How* to choose our future reality and resolve the quandary posed by the September 11 events. Are you ready?

CHAPTER IX

Unveiling the Mystery of Mysteries

"There is now incontrovertible evidence that we have entered upon the greatest period of change the world has ever known. The ills from which we are suffering have had their seat in the very foundation of human thought. But today something is happening to the whole structure of human consciousness. A fresh kind of life is starting. We are the children of transition, not yet fully conscious of the new powers that have been unleashed: There is for us in the future not only survival but superlife."

— PIERRE TEILHARD DE CHARDIN
1881-1955

"Into the innermost circle have you come, into the mystery of mysteries..."
— THE ESSENE GOSPEL OF PEACE BOOK 4
The Teachings of the Elect - pg 41

"The Law was planted to reward the children of light with healing and abundant peace, with long life, with fruitful seed of everlasting blessings, with eternal joy in immortality of eternal Light."
— MANUAL OF DISCIPLINE - DEAD SEA SCROLLS
The Gospel of the Essenes - pg 74

Underlying the premise that "thought creates reality" is a law of nature whose magnitude impacts every realm of existence. This law is referred to as 'The Law of Attraction,' but in a misperception of its scope, potency, and far-reaching ramifications, has held numerous titles over the years such as 'Cause and Effect,' 'Karma,' 'Spiritual Law,' 'Cosmic Law,' etc.

The Law of Attraction states in the most simple of terms: Like energy attracts like energy. Or, in practical terms: whatever we project with our powerful electromagnetic thoughts/feelings/beliefs/actions, our bias, referred to as our "attractor field" in the new science of "Non-linear Dynamics," we will attract into our experience. In the matrix of energy we are a part of, each of our thoughts/feelings/beliefs/actions acts as a boomerang, magnetizing 'evidence' of those thoughts/feelings/beliefs/actions back to us.

"Every prayer — every thought, every statement, every feeling — is creative. To the degree that it is fervently held as truth, to that degree it will be made manifest in your experience."

— NEALE DONALD WALSCH
Conversations with God - Book 1 - pg 12

"Every thought, action, decision, or feeling creates an eddy in the interlocking interbalancing, ever-moving energy fields of life, leaving a permanent record for all of time. This realization can be intimidating when it first dawns on us, but it becomes a springboard for rapid evolution."

— DR. DAVID HAWKINS
Power Versus Force - pg 104

"Let the sons of men who think, speak, and do all good thoughts, words, and deeds inhabit heaven as their home. And let those who think, speak, and do evil thoughts, words, and deeds, abide in chaos....To obtain the treasures of the material world, O sons of men, Forego not the world of the Law...The communions of the Law are perfect, converting the soul from darkness to light."

— THE HOLY LAW
Essene Gospel of Peace - pp 179–181

"The unique human field does not merely react or interact; it transacts because it dynamically makes choices. Here, matter and energy, mind and spirit, are not really different things, only aspects of an expanded reality."

— DR. VALERIE HUNT
Infinite Mind: Science of the Human Vibrations of Consciousness - pg 51

"Hear ye and listen, O my children. Magic is knowledge and only is Law. Be not afraid of the power within thee for it follows Law as the stars in the sky. Follow ye and learn of my magic. Know that all force is thine if thou fear not the path that leads thee to knowledge, but rather shun the dark road. Light is thine, O Man, for the taking. Cast off the fetters and thou shalt be free. Know ye that thy soul is living in bondage fettered by fears that hold ye in thrall. Man is only what he believeth, a brother of darkness or a child of the light."

— THE EMERALD TABLETS OF THOTH - TABLET 12

How are you to know if the information I am conveying is valid? Truth resonates in your heart. Truth can be defined as that which empowers and unifies humanity.

"The heart knows truth as that which sets it free."

— GLENDA GREEN
Love Without End: Jesus Speaks - pg 56

"It is the heart, and not the brain that to the highest doth attain. And he who followeth Love's behest, far excelleth all the rest!"

— HENRY WADSWORTH LONGFELLOW
1807-1882

"There are no new Truths, but only Truths that have not been recognized by those who have perceived them without noticing."

— MARY MCCARTHY
1912-1989

"What is Truth? For the same things appear different to different minds, and even to the same mind at different times. What then is Truth?... To men is Truth revealed according to their capacity to understand and receive. The one truth hath many sides, and one seeth one side only, another another, and some see more than others, according as it is given to them....That which appeareth true to some, seemeth not true to others. They who are in the valley see not as they who are on the hilltop. But to each, it is the truth as the one mind seeth, and for that time, till a higher truth shall be revealed unto the same; and to the soul which receiveth higher light, shall be given more light."

— THE GOSPEL OF THE HOLY TWELVE
The Essene New Testament - pg 151

"There are joys which long to be ours. God sends ten thousand truths, which come about us like birds seeking inlet; but we are shut up to them, and so they bring us nothing but sit and sing awhile upon the roof, and then fly away."

— HENRY WARD BEECHER
1813-1887

"And I will ask the Father, and He will give you another counselor to be with you forever — the Spirit of truth. The world cannot accept Him, because it neither sees Him nor knows Him. But you know Him, for He lives with you and will be in you."

— THE BIBLE
John 14:16-17

"There is nothing so powerful as 'Truth' — and often nothing so strange."

— DANIEL WEBSTER
1782-1852

"It is only with the heart that one can see rightly; what is essential is invisible to the eye."
— ANTOINE DE SAINT-EXUPERY
1900-1944

"Man will occasionally stumble upon the truth, but most of the time he will pick himself up and continue on."
— WINSTON CHURCHILL
1874-1965

Knowledge is the first step in choosing our future reality. Therefore, we must open our eyes and accept that aspects of life, heretofore not fully understood, do indeed exist. The question is: Are we ready to accept this more expansive version of truth?

"...human inquiry can continue indefinitely to yield important new truths."
— HENRY STAPP
The Copenhagen Interpretation and the Nature of Space-Time
American Journal of Physics, 40, 1972, 1098ff

"In our time, what is at issue is the very nature of humankind, the image we have of our limits and possibilities. History is not yet done with its exploration of the limits of what it means to be human."
— C. WRIGHT MILLS
1914-1962

Let's now explore the basic tenets of the Law of Attraction for then we will begin to see how this law underlies our every experience in life.

 CHAPTER X

The Time Has Come to Advance Our Thoughts

"Of all the creatures of Earth, only human beings can change their pattern. Man alone is the architect of his destiny. The greatest revolution in our generation is that of human beings, by changing the inner attitudes of their minds, can change the outer aspects of their lives."

— WILLIAM JAMES
1942-1910

"We are in the early morning of understanding our place in the universe and our spectacular latent powers, the flexibility and transcendence of which we are capable."

— MARILYN FERGUSON
The Aquarian Conspiracy - pg 279

*"And one day the eyes of your spirit shall open
and you shall know all things."*
— THE ESSENE GOSPEL OF PEACE

*"Those who had premonitions of transformation
believed that future generations might detect the
invisible laws and forces around us; the vital
networks of relationship, the ties among all
aspects of life and knowledge, the interweaving
of people, the rhythms and harmonies of the
universe, the connectedness that captures parts
and makes them wholes, the patterns that draw
meaning from the web of the world. Humankind,
they said, might recognize the subtle veils
imposed on seeing; might awaken to screens of
custom, the prison of language and culture, the
bonds of circumstance."*
— MARILYN FERGUSON
The Aquarian Conspiracy - pg 46

Before utilizing our new awareness of the Law of
Attraction to formulate a solution to the crisis posed
by September 11, let's delve deeper into the basic
tenets of this Law so that we have a thorough
understanding of how it operates.

From this point forward we must leave science
behind, for until it can accept the expanded version
of 'cause and effect,' essentially transcending its
current dogma, it will continue to play the role of the
hamster on the wheel going 'round and 'round, but
going nowhere. We must now rely upon our own life
experience for proof, for it is only when each of us,
individually, discovers the correlation between our

thoughts/beliefs/words/actions and life experiences, that we find the Law of Attraction not only plausible, but blindingly conspicuous.

> *"Know ye, O man, that all that exists is only an aspect of greater things to come. Matter is fluid and flows like a stream, constantly changing from one thing to another. The key to worlds within thee, is found only within, for man is the gateway of mystery, and the key is that One is within One."*
> — ADAPTED FROM THE EMERALD TABLETS OF THOTH

> *"As perception itself evolves with one's level of consciousness, it becomes apparent that what the world calls the domain of causes is, in fact, the domain of effects. By taking responsibility for the consequences of his own perceptions, the observer can transcend the role of victim to an understanding that 'nothing out there has power over you'."*
> — DR. DAVID HAWKINS
> *Power Versus Force - pp 55–56*

THE LAW OF ATTRACTION AT WORK

Whenever we focus on a specific topic, we are, in that moment, projecting the energy of our electromagnetic thoughts and beliefs, our bias, onto that topic, thus drawing it to us and adding unto it. If we continue to focus on that topic, we will contribute more and more energy (matter) to it, until it culminates in a physical manifestation — a person, event, object, or circumstance.

To illustrate how the Law of Attraction works quietly under the cover of life, I'd like to share a paraphrased version of a true story I discovered in *A Fourth Course of Chicken Soup for the Soul* entitled *"To Save a Life"* by Hanoch McCarty:

> *Just after World War II ended in the late 1940's, an immigrant family in New York tried to contact their relatives in Hungary. They wondered if their family was still alive; if they had survived the war. But communications were sporadic and the mails untrustworthy. It could take weeks, even months for letters to travel to Europe and just as long for replies to return.*
>
> *Happily, the day finally arrived when the New York family received a letter from their Uncle Lazlo, who lived in a small town near Budapest. Miraculously, their relatives had survived the war, but it was clear that they were hungry and hurting. Food and other necessities were in short supply, the currency nearly valueless, and the black market thriving. Critical infrastructures; electrical plants, water supply, and fuel reserves had been decimated in the unrelenting bombing, making everyday life extremely difficult.*
>
> *Concerned about the plight of their relatives, the New Yorkers decided to send 'care packages' — items that would be useful in a postwar*

situation. They stuffed cartons to the brim with canned meats, vegetables, chocolates, toilet paper, bandages, candies, paper, pencils, or anything else they could think of, and sent them off to Budapest.

When a few months passed and they heard nothing though, the New Yorkers began to worry. Movie theaters, the only source of news on the European front, played newsreels that revealed emaciated Europeans walking down rubble-strewn streets in a daze as they dodged numerous bomb craters. Headlines added even more fuel to their distress, for stories abounded about people starving to death. On top of all that, a historically severe winter was reported to be on the horizon. The silence was agonizing.

Finally another letter arrived from Uncle Lazlo. 'My Dearest Cousins; We are so grateful for the packages you sent. Food is so scarce here....' The letter went on to discuss almost every item in the cartons and the uses to which they had been put. But then came a mystery.... 'We also cannot thank you enough for the medicine you sent. It is so difficult to get medicine now and often it is of poor potency. Cousin Gesher's knees were so swollen and painful that he was only able to walk with the use of a cane, but your medicine has miraculously cured him! My back pain is completely gone, as are Lizabeta's migraine headaches, and Anna's continual fevers. America is great and its science is great! But our medicine is almost gone. Could you please send more?'

The family in New York looked at one another quizzically. What medicine was Uncle Lazlo talking about? Immediately, they drafted a letter asking Uncle Lazlo to provide the name of the medicine so urgently needed.

Two months later a reply arrived: 'My Dearest Cousins; We are grateful to have heard from you once more. Again, you sent that wonderful medicine. And since it did not come with instructions, we guessed at the dosage. Translating from English to Hungarian is difficult since only young Sandor has studied it in school. Luckily he could translate the name of the medicine. It is 'Life Savers®.' Please send more as soon as you can. Love, Lazlo.' pp 231–235

Okay, were you aware of the medicinal benefit of LifeSavers®? Probably not. Because you *believe* that LifeSavers® are *candy,* that's the reality you will experience. However, because Uncle Lazlo and family didn't "know any better," they believed, or *assumed* (key word here, for their assumptions exposed their bias) that this *candy* was medicine. And lo and behold, the power of their thoughts created a reality where 'candy' was able to cure a variety of ailments.

This story vividly illustrates what is referred to as the *"placebo effect,"* which in Greek means "to please." However, there is another more ominous element to the power of belief called the *nocebo* effect. So, let's explore another paraphrased passage, one that vividly illustrates the nocebo effect. This passage is from *Timeless Healing: The Power and Biology of Belief* by Dr. Herbert Benson, founder of the Harvard Mind Body Institute in Boston.

At the turn of the century, Dr. Walter Cannon, a renowned physiologist on staff at the Harvard Medical School, studied the Maori aborigines in New Zealand, a culture that believed in the power of taboo. Taboo was utilized by the tribal hierarchy as a punishment when an individual committed a forbidden act. A 'hex,' or 'magic spell,' would be placed upon the offender that was believed to be so powerful, it would evoke a fatal terror in its victim culminating in death. Dr. Cannon's research included the following story that addressed the prophetic power of taboo:

> *While traveling, a young aborigine stayed at the home of an older friend. For breakfast the elder served a meal containing wild hen — a food forbidden, thus taboo, to the younger generation. Suspecting that this bird might be wild hen, the young man questioned his host several times, but each time the elder man assured him that it was not. A few years later, the friends reunited and the older man asked the younger if he would now eat wild hen. The young man replied that of course he would not because it was forbidden. The elder man then laughed, explaining that years earlier he had tricked him into eating the*

hen and nothing terrible had happened as he believed. Upon receiving this news, however, the young man became extremely distressed. In fact, he was in so much physical torment that within twenty-four hours he was dead. pp 40–41

As you can clearly see, there is something very powerful working beneath the surface of life experience, and that something is called the Law of Attraction.

"Belief can...work against us. The brain/body does digest unpleasant images and can fulfill ugly prophecies."
— DR. HERBERT BENSON
Timeless Healing: The Power and Biology of Belief - pg 39

"Our brains are wired for beliefs and expectancies. When activated, the body can respond as it would if the belief were a reality, producing deafness or thirst, health or illness."
— DR. HERBERT BENSON
Timeless Healing: The Power and Biology of Belief - pp 63 & 39

What does this information mean in a practical sense? At the extreme end of the spectrum, if a doctor tells you that you have only months to live because you have developed an 'incurable' disease and you *believe* him or her, you will experience that reality. However, you now know that the doctors' response is but one potential *out of many*. Therefore, the question posed to you is: What probability would you prefer? What reality do you *wish* to create?

"In 1979, Dr. Benson and his colleague Dr. David P. McCallie Jr. reviewed a long history of therapies designed to alleviate angina pectoris — pain in the chest and arms caused by decreased blood flow to the muscle of the heart. The treatments, ranging from injections of cobra venom to surgeries to remove the thyroid or parts of the pancreas, were enthusiastically introduced medical practice years ago even though today we know they were misguided. But despite there being no physiologic reason these techniques should have worked, they often did. When these ersatz techniques were used and believed in, they were effective 70 to 90 percent of the time, working two to three times more often than doctors had said they would. And interestingly, later, when physicians began to doubt whether these treatments worked, their effectiveness dropped to 30 to 40 percent."

— DR. HERBERT BENSON
Timeless Healing: The Power and Biology of Belief - pg 30

"Take the case of 2000 men who were treated with beta-blocking drugs after having heart attacks. It turned out that doubts or negative beliefs, translated into actions, helped to determine whether they lived or died."

— DR. HERBERT BENSON
Timeless Healing: The Power and Biology of Belief - pg 44

"[W]e should not ignore compelling brain research that demonstrates that beliefs manifest themselves throughout our bodies."

— DR. HERBERT BENSON
Timeless Healing: The Power and Biology of Belief - pg 30

"The medical system is in crisis... and the best remedy of all may lie in...[the] yet untapped resources that our brilliant brains and visceral souls make possible."

— DR. HERBERT BENSON
Timeless Healing: The Power and Biology of Belief - pg 95

"[W]e are, without a doubt, at a turning point in the history of belief in healing. As medical researchers, we expect some exceptions and anomalies from our statistics. But the finding that patients who consistently follow doctor's orders, believing that doing so would make them well, were twice as likely to live, is sobering."

— DR. HERBERT BENSON
Timeless Healing: The Power and Biology of Belief - pg 45

"For you know not the power of your thoughts. Know, Sons of Light, that your thoughts are as powerful as the bolt of lightning that stabs through the storm and splits asunder the mighty tree... Use, then, wisdom in all you think, and say, and do... May the Law bless you with all good and keep you from all evil, and illumine your hearts with insight into the things of life, and grace you with knowledge of things' Eternal."

— THE ESSENE GOSPEL OF PEACE BOOK 4
The Teachings of the Elect - pp 16–17

Thought has both tremendous power and far-reaching ramifications, therefore it is imperative that we now learn to use our thoughts to our advantage.

BASIS TENETS OF THE LAW OF ATTRACTION

"Enlighten the people generally, and tyranny and oppressions of body and mind will vanish like evil spirits at the dawn of day."
— THOMAS JEFFERSON
1743-1826

Let's now apply this information to the crisis at hand. If we focus on terrorism, guess what we will magnetize into our experience? MORE terrorism, for the Law of Attraction states:

WHATEVER WE FOCUS ON OR FEAR, WE WILL MAGNETIZE INTO OUR EXPERIENCE.

"[A] society [or a person] living in fear, very often — actually, inevitably — produces in form that which it fears most."
— NEALE DONALD WALSCH
Conversations with God - Book 1 - pg 55

To better understand how the Law of Attraction works, think of every topic in the world encoded with a specific frequency. Whenever you focus your powerful magnetic thoughts on a particular topic, you are attuning to its frequency, and will begin to attract it into your experience, whether you want it or not, for the Law of Attraction states:

WHATEVER WE PUSH AGAINST, WE ATTRACT.

> *"The act of resisting a thing is the act of granting it life... the more you resist, the more you make it real — whatever it is you are resisting."*
>
> — NEALE DONALD WALSCH
> *Conversations with God - Book 1 - pg 102*

In other words, if you focus on *not* wanting war, you will instead *attract* or perpetuate it! Why? *"I want peace"* indicates that peace is not present, revealing that you are attuned to the *'lack of peace'* frequency, thereby attracting circumstances that exist at that frequency. Therefore, it is imperative to understand that the underlying feeling you project, your *intention*, bias, or belief — the feeling *underlying* the thought, referred to as the sponsoring thought — determines what will manifest. So, the trick is to focus on and *intend* what is *wanted*, peace, and then to project its frequency — what it *feels* like to live in peace as if you already were. Like energy will then attract more like energy because the Law of Attraction states:

> *WHATEVER WE GIVE OUR ATTENTION TO GROWS LARGER.*

> *"Successful solutions are based on the powerful principle that resolution occurs not by attacking the negative, but by fostering the positive."*
>
> — DR. DAVID HAWKINS
> *Power Versus Force - pg 139*

Think in terms of *attention* and *intention*. Your attention to a specific topic will begin to draw it to you and your intention will determine what *aspect* of that topic you will experience. Let's take that concept a step further. Every topic in our world has polar opposites with a vast spectrum of frequencies or probabilities between its two poles. In your mind's eye, imagine every topic having a radio dial — one you are capable of adjusting with your intentions. Your *intention,* essentially your bias, determines which 'station' you tune into, or probability you will actualize, whenever you focus on a particular topic.

For example: Money is a common subject that most of us focus on. If you think/believe/feel that you have too little money, you will magnetize people/events/circumstances that will validate your belief, for that is the 'station' you are tuned in to. However, because you have the ability to *consciously* choose your thoughts, you can change stations, or actualize the probability you prefer! So, to magnetize more money, you would begin to project a different frequency, what it *feels* like to *have* money right now. And as that frequency becomes more dominant than your previous frequency, you will attract people/events/circumstances, evidence of *that* frequency in your experience, for you have tuned into a new station.

> "*Any mind which accepts its power completely and can focus thought can do profound things. The mind on the nonphysical level has eminent power.*"
>
> — DR. VALERIE HUNT
> *Infinite Mind: Science of the Human Vibrations of Consciousness - pg 99*

INNER GUIDANCE SYSTEM

"Make [your] future dream a present fact by assuming the feeling of [your] desire fulfilled."
— NEVILLE GODDARD
1905-1972 The Power of Awareness - pg 10

"Quite deliberately, you use your conscious mind playfully, creating a game as children do, in which for a time you completely ignore what seems to be real in physical terms and 'pretend' that what you want is real."
— JANE ROBERTS
The Nature of Personal Reality - A Seth Book - pg 63

If you are thinking, "This is waaaay too much work. Constantly monitor my thoughts to make sure they are focused in the right direction? I don't think so...." But fear not. When you were born, you came equipped with an inner guidance system, and one of its functions is to warn you when your thoughts are focused in the wrong direction. Just as your physical body warns you of a threat to its well being through physical pain, your emotional body warns you of a threat to its well being through emotional pain — bad feelings.

Your guidance system works very simply. If you *feel* good, you are focused on a topic that is aligned with your comfort zone, programming, or meme, and you will attract more of what you are focused on — a good thing. However, when you feel bad, your thoughts are focused on a topic that is *not* aligned with the contents of your comfort zone, and if you continue to focus on it, you will attract more of it — not a good thing. What you *do* in a 'bad' moment determines your future experience, for a 'bad' feeling indicates a 'wrong-way' sign. Your guidance system is alerting you to a 'choice point,' a *Point of Power*. In this moment, it would be wise to shift your thoughts, or 'change stations,' and you do that by first determining what you *want*. This should be relatively easy for when you know what you *don't* want, you can more easily determine what you *do* want.

> *"Feeling good is your way of telling yourself that your last thought was truth, that your last word was wisdom, that your last action was love."*
> — NEALE DONALD WALSCH
> *Conversations with God - Book 2 - pg 80*

To magnetize what you want, you simply tune into its frequency by *imagining* what it *feels* like to have it. As you project this new feeling frequency, you are 'changing stations,' consciously shifting your bias — essentially choosing the future reality you prefer. Next, you will begin to attract people, events, or circumstances that are aligned with the new frequency you are now projecting.

"Without this playing of fantasy no creative work has ever come to birth. The debt we owe to the play of imagination is incalculable."

— CARL JUNG
1875-1961

"When unto thee there comes a feeling that draws thee nearer to the dark gate, examine thine heart to know if the feeling has come from within. Send through the body a wave of vibration, irregular at first, regular at second, repeating time after time until free. Start the wave force in the brain center. Direct in waves from thine head to thy foot."

— THE EMERALD TABLETS OF THOTH - TABLET 12

The Law of Attraction is unwavering in its simplicity and execution. You are using it in your every moment. You just didn't know it. However, it's time that we, as humankind, now use it to evolve.

"God giveth you all Truth as a ladder with many steps for the salvation and perfection of the soul, and the truth which seemeth today, ye will abandon for the higher truth of the morrow....As I [Jesus] have received the Truth, so I have given it to you. Let each receive it according to their light and ability to understand, and persecute not those who receive it after a different interpretation."

— THE GOSPEL OF THE HOLY TWELVE
The Essene New Testament - pg 152

Before applying this information to the quandary posed by September 11, let's explore one last important piece of the 'puzzle of life,' a piece that is impacting life at this very moment, and intensifying the need to begin utilizing our authentic power.

CHAPTER XI

Geophysical Earth Changes
and their Effects

"We are living the completion of a cycle that began nearly 200,000 years ago, and a process of initiation that was demonstrated over 2,000 years ago... We are living in a global initiation chamber, with...geophysical changes occurring on a worldwide scale. It is as if Earth herself is preparing us for the next stage of evolution."

— GREGG BRADEN
Awakening to Zero Point: The Collective Initiation - pg viii

Another aspect of the "Shift of the Ages" that is currently impacting life is geophysical Earth changes. One of the changes now occurring concerns the magnetic frequency of Earth, referred to by some as her heartbeat and to the scientific community as the "Schumann Resonance" (quasi-standing electromagnetic waves that dwell in the cavity between the surface of the Earth and the inner edge of the ionosphere 55 kilometers high). First measured in 1898, Earth's frequency consistently calibrated at 7.25–7.8Hz, therefore it was assumed to be a given, a constant, for it never wavered. In fact, science was so assured of its viability that in the International Geophysical year of 1958, this base frequency was adopted for both satellite and military communications by much of the world. However, most notably in the mid-1980's, this frequency began to increase. And by May of 1997 it had risen to 10–11Hz,* and continues to increase today — just as the prophecies indicated.

What are the implications of this increase? Many and vast. Metaphysicists tell us that as Earth's frequency increases, the speed by which energy magnetizes matter increases as well. Now this can be the good news and the bad news, depending on where your thoughts are focused. For *whatever* you focus on, good or bad, you're gonna magnetize evidence — people, events, or circumstances — of those thoughts rather quickly in your experience. Therefore, when you encounter aspects of life that *feel* bad, it is of utmost importance to 'turn your cheek,' refocus your powerful thoughts from what you don't want so that you don't attract *more* of it. In those moments, it would be of great value to employ your 'Point of Power' so that you can magnetize what you want.

*(Handbooks of Atmospheric Electrodynamics Volume 1, Chapter 11, Hans Volland ©1995 Published by CRC Press).

In this state of accelerated energy, time seems to 'fly by,' which is what the Ancients were referring to when they spoke of 'the end of time.' However, without an awareness of this knowledge, you can easily see how problems will grow larger and more vast in a shorter period of time. Life will resemble the famous first lines from Dicken's *"A Tale of Two Cities"*:

> *"It was the best of times and it was the worst of times, it was the age of wisdom, it was the age of incredulity, it was the season of light, it was the season of darkness, it was the spring of hope, it was the darkness of despair, we had everything before us, we had nothing before us, we were all going direct to Heaven, we were all going direct the other way..."*
>
> — CHARLES DICKENS
> *1812-1870*

The crevasse between the 'haves' and 'have-nots' will not only grow wider, but intensify *unless* we make the correlation between our thoughts/feelings/words/actions and life experiences. Indeed what we *sow*, we're gonna reap — fast. That is why this information is so critical.

> *"Man is immobilized in his present condition by his alignment with enormously powerful attractor energy patterns which he himself sets unconsciously in motion."*
>
> — DR. DAVID HAWKINS
> *Power Versus Force - pg 22*

REPRESSED ENERGY WILL EXPLODE
SOONER OR LATER

Okay, so here we are immersed in a sea of energy, not having a clue as to the effects of what we do or don't do in each moment, so up until this point in time we have created beaucoup chaos. For denied feelings/thoughts/actions/words don't just 'go away.' As the Law of Conservation states: "Energy cannot be created nor destroyed." Nor can energy remain in a state of imbalance — it will always seek balance. Therefore, any unpleasant past issues that we have tried to 'sweep under the rug,' hoping they would magically disappear, can only come back to bite us! For an imbalance in energy *remains* in our energy fields as "stuck ch'i" (energy that has not been emoted or expressed. Emotion = energy in motion), and will attract more and more of the same energy until this accumulation of energy eventually culminates in a physical manifestation.

As we learned earlier, an energy imbalance will first manifest as smaller adverse incidents, indicating the need to pay attention to something that has become 'stuck' — something we are either denying, have forgotten, or 'put on the back burner.' To regain our equilibrium with the least amount of pain, we must uncover the source of the issue and resolve it. For if we fail to heed the 'wrong-way' signs given, the repressed energy that was created will continue to build until a crisis of magnitude manifests, thereby *forcing* the expression of the repressed energy.

In the majority of cases, the manifestation of illness is a result of unexpressed or unresolved emotion — a quandary having no viable solution within a person's current comfort zone. Because this 'stuck' energy cannot be destroyed, whatever is not expressed outwardly will express inwardly. This premise has long been known in the Chinese culture that has believed, for more than two thousand years, that all illness is created by 'stuck ch'i' — energy in a state of imbalance, energy that has not been expressed.

Think in terms of a pressure cooker: As more and more steam (energy) builds within the pot, it creates a potentially explosive condition. If you don't take the pressure cooker off the stove (remove your thoughts from a topic that evokes 'bad' feelings), or fail to release some of the accumulated steam (emote the energy of a circumstance), that sucker is going to 'blow.' And we see evidence of this form of repressed energy manifesting daily in road rage, plane rage, 'going postal,' the Rodney King incident, school shootings, etc. Every one of those incidents is, or was, simply an accumulation of energy that 'blew,' or manifested.

Think about a child who is teased and tormented by peers, or disciplined through fear, power, and dominance. If this child does nothing to emote the inevitable anger, resentment, and desire for vengeance created, the repressed energy will simply magnetize more of the same energy. The result? The child becomes a ticking time bomb ready to explode when the next incident aligned with that energy frequency pushes his/her 'button.' Therefore, if we do not become familiar with how energy transacts in life, tragic incidents will become more and more prevalent until people are shouting out of their windows: *"I'm mad as hell and I'm not going to take it any more"* — thus expressing *their* pent-up energy.

The bottom line? Nothing in life 'just happens.' *Nothing* is an accident. There is no such thing as a 'coincidence.' The Law of Attraction is underlying every occurrence in life, so it's time we learn to use it to our advantage. And now the stakes are high. Confronted with a crisis of enormous magnitude, we must begin to utilize this knowledge so we can move into the future with hope, empowerment, and a sense of direction.

∽

How are you feeling right now? Overwhelmed? If so, that's a normal reaction, for this information challenges the prevailing beliefs of humankind, literally impelling a paradigm shift of enormous magnitude — becoming aware of the power of your thoughts. Keep in mind though, once you move beyond 'paradigm-shock,' this information essentially says that you are one powerful dude, and the only limitations you have in life are those you impose upon yourself!

∽

This chapter contributes the final piece to the 'puzzle of life,' and concludes Part I of this book. So, now that you have a foundation of understanding, let's move onto the second part of the book: Applying this knowledge to the crisis imposed by September 11.

CHAPTER XII

Arriving at a 'Soulution' Layer by Layer

"By your choice dwell you now in the world which you have created. What you hold in your heart shall be true, and what most you admire, that shall you become. Fear not, nor be dismayed at the appearance that is darkness, at the disguise that is evil, at the empty cloak that is death, for you have picked these for your challenges. They are the stones on which you whet the keen edge of your spirit. Know that ever about you stands the reality of love, and in each moment you have the power to transform your world by what you have learned."

— RICHARD BACH
One - pg 150

Now that you have a more expansive awareness of the 'bigger picture' of life, who you really are and how life operates at the most fundamental levels of existence, we can begin to utilize our authentic power to formulate a 'soulution' to the crisis presented by the tragic events of September 11. Before we begin though, let's review what we have covered:

1. We are all students in a schoolroom called Earth.

2. Evolution is the name of the game.

3. Each person on this planet is engaged in a specific meme, or stage of development, indicating their level of experience, cognitive capacity, and consciousness.

4. Each of us has created a unique comfort zone based on our specific meme, programming, and life experiences.

5. If we evolve too rapidly in one area of our being — body/mind/spirit — personally or collectively, an imbalance will result. This imbalance will manifest as smaller adverse incidents, alerting us to this predicament.

6. If these smaller incidents are ignored, the unexpressed energy will continue building until it manifests into a larger crisis, thus illuminating our imbalance to an even greater degree. This allows us

another opportunity to resolve the underlying issue
— the cause responsible for creating the imbalance.

7. A grave threat exists to our planet and humankind because science and technology are unaware of the Law of Attraction. Because the intentions of scientists, or those who hire them, are often based on an 'us versus them' belief or bias, rather than the betterment of humanity, the probability of destroying mankind and our world is the most dominant probability that exists today.

8. We, as humankind, have arrived at a critical point in our collective evolution, one where we must utilize the Law of Attraction to *consciously choose* our future reality. The science of Quantum Physics validates the fact that this is feasible.

9. To balance the imbalance created by science and technology, we must employ the knowledge of the Law of Attraction. For that knowledge provides the means to consciously regain our equilibrium, or transmute the negative energy created from our current imbalance to positive, thus actualizing a different probability.

10. Humanity is being tested. In order to move onto the next level of consciousness, we must now leave our comfort zones and acknowledge our 'stuck ch'i' — our past repressed issues — so that we can clean out our energy fields and regain our equilibrium.

The question now posed to us is: Will we have the wisdom and fortitude to change, or will we tenaciously cling to our current beliefs, impelling a repetition of this lesson?

"Past experiences are a source of wisdom"
— CEANNE DeROHAN
The Right Use of Will - pg 193

"Our consciousness is the result of our own choosing. Where you are is where you have come. Where you will go is decided by how you are."
— JON PENIEL
The Lost Teachings of Atlantis - pg 127

"For most of your life you've lived at the effect of your experiences. Now, you're invited to be the cause of them. That is what is known as conscious living. That is what is called walking in awareness."
— NEALE DONALD WALSCH
Conversations with God - Book 1 - pg 156

"We, the generation that faces the next century, can add the ...solemn injunction, 'If we don't do the impossible, we shall be faced with the unthinkable."
— PETRA KELLY
1947-1991 founder of the German Green Party

"We have had our last chance. If we do not devise some greater and more equitable system, Armageddon will be at our door."
— GENERAL DOUGLAS MAC ARTHUR
1880-1964 - September 2, 1945

"Man is not made by his circumstances, he is revealed by them."

— JAMES ALLEN
1849-1925 As a Man Thinketh - pg 16

"The world view that has dominated western civilization has given us tremendous progress, but it cannot be said to have given us peace...No matter how much some people might try to hold back the tide of change today, the remedies of the materialistic order will have less and less effect on affairs now unfolding. The chaos of our times is a reflection of a profound and inexorable reorientation of the human mind. This explosion is coming from the deepest levels of the psyche: it is not orderly, and no amount of tight repressive force can contain it. We can no more stop its energy than a parent can stop the explosion of hormones in an adolescent child. This trans-formation of human consciousness is — it is not up for a vote. No action — only principle — can govern chaos. Our lives will not be brought to order through anything but love."

— MARIANNE WILLIAMSON
The Healing of America - pp 38–39

Let's now employ our newly discovered knowledge and explore a new-paradigm soulution to the quandary we face. Because the issues before us are multifaceted, their soulution must be as well. The terrorist element of the events of September 11, although of utmost importance because of its potential to cause great harm, is simply the surface manifestation — the *effect* of a cause or imbalance that lies at a deeper level of consciousness. Therefore, it is imperative that we uncover this *cause* so we can transmute the energy it is projecting from negative to positive.

A NEW-PARADIGM RESPONSE TO THE ATTACKS OF SEPTEMBER 11

Part 1: *ERADICATING TERRORISM* — Taking the matches away from the children before they burn down the house.

Part 2: *ACHIEVING PEACE THROUGH AUTHENTIC POWER* — Utilizing the Law of Attraction to empower ourselves and achieve a lasting peace.

Part 3: *SELF-CONFRONTATION* — *CLEANING UP OUR OWN BACKYARD* — Transmuting the energy of our suppressed experiences through an examination of our collective 'shadow' self.

Part 4: *LIVING AT THE NEXT LEVEL OF CONSCIOUSNESS* — Utilizing our authentic power to improve the quality of life, alleviate unnecessary pain, and recreate our world by actualizing the "Heaven on Earth" probability.

Let's now examine each of these soulutions more thoroughly.

CHAPTER XIII

Soulution Part 1:
Eradicating Terrorism

"*By objectifying, controlling, and demystifying the external world, the dominant scientific paradigm has reinforced the ancient barricade between order and chaos... This modern version of the primordial human fear, that order must be fortified against the ever-present threat of annihilation by chaos, is why bombs are stock-piled; why political regimes suppress freedoms; why our shadow gets projected onto others; why our ego defenses alienate others; and why we resist change.*"

— MOIRA TIMMS
Beyond Prophecies and Predictions - pg 24

OLD-PARADIGM FORCE VERSUS
NEW-PARADIGM POWER

Part I of our soulution deals with eradicating terrorism. Rather than simply adopting the old-paradigm approach of killing one's enemy, the method habitually employed throughout history, we must now be cognizant of the Law of Attraction and its repercussions. The following quotations admonish us to be aware of our thoughts/feelings/words/actions/decisions — to consider the magnetic intent underlying them:

"You may feel quite virtuous in hating evil, or what seems to you to be evil; but if you find yourself concentrating upon either hatred or evil, you are creating it."

— JANE ROBERTS
The Nature of Personal Reality- A Seth book - pg 31

"Do not judge, and you will not be judged. Do not condemn, and you will not be condemned. Forgive, and you will be forgiven. Give, and it will be given to you. For with the measure you use, it will be measured to you."

— THE BIBLE
Luke 6:37-38

"Those who would lead us into cynicism or anger, lead us away from healing."

— MARIANNE WILLIAMSON
The Healing of America - pg 24

"[J]udge not, and neither condemn, for you know not why a thing occurs, nor to what end. And remember you this: that which you condemn, will condemn you, and that which you judge, you will one day become. Rather, seek to change those things — or support others who are changing those things — which no longer reflect your highest sense of Who You Are."

— NEALE DONALD WALSCH
Conversations with God - Book 1 - pg 38

"That which we call sin in others is experiment for us."

— RALPH WALDO EMERSON
1803-1882

"No man is your enemy, no man is your friend, every man is your teacher."

— UNKNOWN

Our knee-jerk reaction to the horrific events of September 11 was to respond as we always have; in anger and vengeance — at our present level of consciousness. However, because the intricate webs of treachery that the terrorists have woven cannot be unraveled overnight, we have been afforded ample time to employ a new-paradigm soulution.

Rather than advocating a pacificist response that the Taliban, or any organization in a more primary meme, would welcome and regard as irresolute on our part, the question is not "*Do* we stop terrorism," but "*How* do we stop terrorism." And the answer is, once more, multi-faceted.

First and foremost, we must stop 'the children' and take away the matches, for if we don't, they'll burn down the entire house. And it appears that the coalition conceived by the Bush Administration is doing just that. However, at the same time, we must utilize the Law of Attraction to formulate a soulution that acknowledges the *effects* of our actions. We must respond with *wisdom* to the deep-seated issues that *created* the terrorists — the underlying cause. And just what is wisdom? The translation of knowledge into action — knowledge that lies at the next level of awareness.

OLD PARADIGM = FORCE: TO DESTROY ANOTHER IS TO MAGNETIZE SELF-DESTRUCTION

"Truly each thought of darkness, whether it be of malice or anger or vengeance, these wreak destruction like that of fire sweeping through dry kindling under a windless sky. But man does not see the carnage, nor does he hear the piteous cries of his victims, for he is blind to the world of the spirit."

— THE ESSENE GOSPEL OF PEACE - BOOK 4
The Teachings of the Elect - pg 32

Much wisdom has been passed onto us regarding how *to* and how *not* to resolve issues.

> *"When sophisticated weapons of mass destruction are in the hands of many, war [and even armed conflict altogether] ceases to be something that can be 'won.' The governments of the world are, in general, acting as if they do not understand or accept this current reality. Since the twentieth century, war itself has become a threat to all of humankind — not merely the parties directly involved in any particular conflict."*
>
> — ADI DA SAMRAJ
> *The Peace Law*

> *"An eye for an eye, leaves everyone blind."*
>
> — MARTIN LUTHER KING, JR.
> *1929-1968*

> *"I know not with what weapons World War III will be fought, but World War IV will be fought with sticks and stones."*
>
> — ALBERT EINSTEIN
> *1879-1955*

War eliminates the *effect* of an issue, the surface element, but fails to address the cause. Therefore, if the elimination of terrorism is our *only* response to the attacks of September 11, we will only create a vicious circle. Since like energy attracts like energy, the energy created by war creates a 'tit-for-tat' condition — you hurt me, I'll hurt you, you hurt me, I'll hurt you etc. The result? We become the proverbial hamster running 'round and 'round the wheel going nowhere. In addition, the imbalance remains, thus ensuring continual adversarial circumstances. (Republicans versus Democrats…).

> *"Man is stuck with his lack of knowledge about himself until he can learn to look beyond apparent causes. From the human record we may note that answers never arise from identifying 'causes' in the world. Instead it is necessary to identify the conditions that underlie the ostensible causes; and these conditions exist only within man's consciousness itself. No definitive answer to any problem can be found by isolating sequences of events and projecting them upon a mental notion of 'causality'."*
>
> — DR. DAVID HAWKINS
> *Power Versus Force - pg 19*

> *"Society constantly expends its efforts to correct effects rather than causes, which is one reason why the evolution of human consciousness proceeds so slowly."*
>
> — DR. DAVID HAWKINS
> *Power Versus Force - pg 19*

Our problem will not be solved by simply eliminating a specific enemy. For the moment that enemy is eliminated, another, we would judge to be even *worse*, will manifest in his place. Why? Because we failed to address the cause. We only eliminated the effect.

"The arrest of a drug kingpin has no effect at all on the drug problem; before he is even jailed he will have been replaced by a new incarnation. In the recent demise of South American drug lord Escobar, he was instantly replaced by three new kingpins, so the hydra now has three heads instead of one."

— DR. DAVID HAWKINS
Power Versus Force - pg 88

The old-paradigm approach to eradicating conflict (old paradigm=current level of awareness) is to apply force; to purge the perceived 'evil' from one's enemy by beating the 'animal' into submission and compliance with superior strength. However, we can now see what will occur if we employ that tactic. We will simply strengthen our adversary's fortitude and galvanize his position that it is *we* who are evil. In the process, we also create our own living hell — the threat of anthrax, smallpox, plane crashes, etc.. Force is clearly ineffective, it only perpetuates conflict, so let's now discuss power, *real* power — the power of thought and how to apply it to the issue at hand.

"The ultimate weakness of violence is that it is a descending spiral, begetting the very thing it seeks to destroy. Instead of diminishing evil, it multiplies it. In fact, violence merely increases hate. Returning violence for violence multiplies violence. Hate cannot drive out hate; only love can do that."

— MARTIN LUTHER KING, JR.
1929-1968

NEW PARADIGM = AUTHENTIC POWER

"Peace cannot be achieved through violence, it can only be attained through understanding."
— ALBERT EINSTEIN

"Condemnation disappears with understanding, as does guilt. All judgement reveals itself to be self-judgement in the end, and when this is understood, a larger comprehension of the nature of life takes place."
— DR. DAVID HAWKINS
Power Versus Force - pg 104

"There is more to be ultimately gained from learning the arts of peace than from perfecting the science of war."
— JAY WALLJASPER

To more fully understand our relationship and responsibility to those at primary levels of con-sciousness, such as the Taliban, let's use the analogy of a parent and child. Who has more responsibility to act judiciously? Obviously a child has not yet gathered enough experience to make wise decisions. He is a product of his 'programming,' and deeply immersed in a particular meme. Therefore, some of the acts of cruelty he inflicts on others, acts we might deem as 'evil,' stem from his current level of consciousness and cognitive capacity. So, how do we handle the terrorists, *these* particular children? Do we allow them to commit evil after evil and chalk it up to "kids will be kids?" No. We have allowed them to escape the consequences of their actions for far too long, and our failure to respond *firmly* and *boldly* to their previous incidents has served to fuel their perception of power and righteousness. They believe that Americans are lazy, irresolute; that we don't care; we don't have the power to stop them; that we've lost our will. But we must bear in mind, they know not what they do for they are at a primary level of consciousness, unaware of the greater truths. Do we punish children for their lack of knowledge or experience? Or do we help them learn from their mistakes and thus expand their consciousness?

We must also consider that oftentimes children have valuable lessons to teach *us*, for they can sometimes see through issues that we, as adults, have become blind to. For example: When I learned that the Taliban wanted to kill Americans because they felt we had lost sight of our spirituality, I was dumbfounded. Forming their perception of us through our television shows, such as *Bay Watch*, they concluded that the American *culture* was decadent — a perception revealing a primary level of consciousness. On the other hand, however, on a deeper level of conscious- ness, they were *feeling* the imbalance in our *collective* being and attempting to achieve equilibrium by eradicating the 'problem' — us. Moreover, in their minds, whatever means they required to achieve their 'righteous' goal would be justified, a response again indicating a primary level of consciousness, and sadly, the most prevalent response used throughout history to 'eradicate' a problem.

"...seek peace with other sons of Men, even with the Pharisees and priests, even with beggars and the homeless, even with kings and governors. For all are Sons of Men, whatever be their station, whatever be their calling, whether their eyes have been opened to see the heavenly kingdoms, or whether they yet walk in darkness and ignorance."

— THE ESSENE GOSPEL OF PEACE - BOOK 4
The Teachings of the Elect - pg 34

If we fail to provide the means to help resolve the underlying imbalances of those at more primary memes, if we fail to extend a helping hand, they *and we* will stagnate at our current levels of consciousness and perpetuate the vicious circle.

We must also bear in mind that the assistance we provide those with ill feelings toward the United States must be geared to their level of awareness. The human mind is linear; it needs a link or bridge that 'connects the dots,' regardless of one's level of consciousness. We must recognize that one will defend his meme to the end, whether that stage of development is scientific, religious, altruistic, mystical, or of a gang-mentality. It is imperative that we continually remind ourselves that we are all sacred souls on a sacred journey of experience, and that our relationships with one another are meant to foster our evolution.

We must also acknowledge that it's natural to want to fight back, it *feels* good because energy is coursing through our beings — momentarily. However, we must get beyond the moment and think long-term. That is, unless we wish to continue 'Playing War' for God knows how many more eons. We must transcend our need for vengeance, and acknowledge what *really* happens in war past the initial adrenaline rush. War is not pretty; it is barbaric.

COACHING WITH AUTHENTIC POWER

Recognizing the inherent futility and inadequacies of force, let's take a look at authentic power using coaching techniques as an example. Many coaches routinely use tactics of force — bullying, threats, fear, power, dominance, intimidation, etc. to 'lead' their teams. And while those methods may be successful in the short-term, in light of our newly-discovered knowledge we must consider: What is the long-term effect of these methods? Because "energy cannot be created nor destroyed," those tactics can only create 'stuck ch'i' in the players which will eventually manifest in one form or another. (spousal or child abuse?)

Now compare that method of coaching to a method that utilizes *authentic power*. Phil Jackson, coach of the world champion Los Angeles Lakers, former coach of the six-time world champion Chicago Bulls, and author of *Sacred Hoops*, has recognized that authentic power, power that resides at higher levels of consciousness — honor, love, and respect — is far more effective than force. By applying the principles and wisdom of Zen Buddhism to basketball, Mr. Jackson has inspired his teams to the extent that they were, and are, able to clinch championship after championship. Higher consciousness recognizes how to utilize the Law of Attraction to one's advantage.

> *"Power arises from meaning. It has to do with motive [intention] and it has to do with principle. Power is always associated with that which supports the significance of life itself. It appeals to that in human nature which we call noble, in contrast to force, which appeals to that which we call crass. Power appeals to that which uplifts and dignifies — ennobles. Force must always be justified, whereas power requires no justification. Force is associated with the partial, power with the whole."*
>
> — DR. DAVID HAWKINS
> *Power Versus Force - pg 108*

The bottom line? The manner in which we respond to this crisis will create energy — good or bad — so we must consider what we will inevitably magnetize back to ourselves.

POWERLESSNESS:
THE ROOT CAUSE OF CONFLICT

> *"If we could read the secret history of our enemies, we should find in each man's life sorrow and suffering enough to disarm all hostility."*
>
> — HENRY W. LONGFELLOW
> *1807-1882*

"The problem is generations of beings who experience not having an identity. The question is: What made human beings incapable of feeling love, compassion, or empathy towards themselves or anyone else, and thereby, becoming destroyers of their own species? What happened that human beings could become so psychologically, emotionally, and spiritually distorted that they could believe that Islam, one of the most spiritual paths in the world, could encourage murder and suicide to gain heavenly reward?"

— UNKNOWN

"People become murderers, robbers, and terrorists because of circumstances and experiences in life. Killing or confining these people is not going to rid this world of them. For every one we kill or confine, we create another hundred to take their place. What we need to do is to analyze dispassionately the circumstances that create such monsters and how we can eliminate those circumstances. Justice should mean reformation, not revenge. We must acknowledge our role in helping to create the monsters in the world and then find ways to contain these monsters without hurting more innocent people. We must move from being respected for our military strength to being respected for our moral strength. We need to appreciate that we are in a position to play a powerful role in helping the 'other half' of the world attain a better standard of life, not by throwing a few crumbs, but by significantly involving ourselves in constructive economic

programs. For too long our foreign policy has been based on 'what is good for the United States.' It smacks of selfishness. Our foreign policy should now be based on what is good for the world and what we can do to help the world become more peaceful."

— ARUN GANDHI
Grandson of Mahatma Gandhi

As we try to understand any adversary, we always find at the core of his or her being, feelings of fear, suffering, and powerlessness — illusions that only exist when one does not understand one's *authentic* power.

"Most criminals [adversaries, bullies, etc.] share a sense of powerlessness and feeling of resentment because of it. Therefore they seek to assure themselves that they are indeed powerful through antisocial acts, often of violence. They desire to be strong, then, while believing in a lack of personal strength. They have been conditioned, and furthermore have conditioned themselves to believe they must fight for any benefits. Aggression becomes a method of survival. Since they believe so strongly in the power of others, and in their own relative powerlessness, they feel forced into aggressive action almost as preventive measures against greater violence that will be done against them."

— JANE ROBERTS
The Nature of Personal Reality - A Seth book - pg 336

Our soulution cannot dismiss a seed of blame, however misguided and illogical we might perceive it to be, that grew and grew until it exploded into the kind of hatred capable of murdering three thousand-forty-four innocent people. It must respectfully examine the ill feelings of some within the MidEast, discover the origin of their animosity, and help to transmute the explosive energy created. Perception is everything, as evidenced by September 11.

> *"[T]he expression of normal aggression prevents the build up of anger into hatred."*
> — JANE ROBERTS
> *The Nature of Personal Reality - A Seth Book - pg 410*

To understand the cause of this tragedy, we must also consider what our adversaries *desire* at the deepest level. We must uncover their fears and feelings of powerlessness. Put yourself in the shoes of a person living in the MidEast. If you observed western cultures infiltrate and homogenize every nook and cranny of the world at such a breakneck speed, perhaps you would fear the extinction of your culture, your history, and everything else that makes you unique.

To uncover our adversary's desires, we would simply ask 'why.' "You don't like Americans?" Why? As we ask 'why' again and again, we peel back layer after layer of programming and expose what is *desired* at the innermost level. Once we have gathered that information, we will then be able to formulate a soulution that addresses those desires and dispels what is feared.

CHILDREN ARE KEY

Another aspect of our soulution must include the psychological perceptions of the children. For how children perceive our response to this atrocity will serve to either perpetuate the conflict, or provide the means to graduate to the next level of consciousness.

Nobel Peace Prize Laureate, Mairead Corrigan Maguire, believes that peace can only be achieved through children. After living through the deaths of her sisters' four children in the Northern Ireland conflict, Ms. McGuire vowed to help put an end to this terrible struggle. She and Betty Williams co-founded the *"Northern Ireland Peace Movement"* which earned them the Nobel Peace Prize in 1976.

In 1998, Benedictine University, in Lisle, Illinois, hosted a forum entitled "Waging Peace in the 21st Century" where Ms. McGuire and three other Nobel Peace Prize Laureates offered their insights. After each spoke individually, they formed a panel to answer questions. When asked: "Do you think peace is attainable in the 21st century?", Ms. Maguire was the only person on the panel who felt that peace *was* possible. However, she felt the key to peace was predicated on understanding and addressing the psyche of a child.

Living in the midst of a terrible conflict, Ms. Maguire could clearly see that the little ones greatly admired those who were older. They believed it was 'cool' to kill or maim the 'enemy;' that they were stamping out the 'bad' guys and 'saving the world.' From their level of consciousness, cognitive capacity, and inexperience, the older generation had become their heroes and their only aspiration in life was to emulate them. So, unless we desire to breed another generation of haters and killers, our soulution must address this impressionable group.

We must leave an indelible mark of humanity on the psyche of the MidEast and engage in a significant campaign of humility and truth, acknowledging that we have indeed made mistakes in the past. We must declare our desire for a dialogue where issues and resentments are respectfully addressed so that *together* we can achieve a lasting peace. The actions we take must induce a shift in underlying perceptions, the cause that triggered this conflict. And if we succeed, as we must, they, and we, will move onto the next meme. To achieve this goal, the onus is on us to take the first step, for those at higher levels of consciousness represent the dominant seat of power, and with that power, have the burden of respon-sibility.

To raise the consciousness of those in the MidEast, it would also be wise to utilize the wisdom of influential Muslim leaders who could address the misinter-pretations of the Qu'ran by the Taliban. Who might these leaders be? An Islamic University professor who was both intelligent and wise — a great role model — was featured on Oprah (another 'Bringer of Light' we have been blessed with). This show, entitled "Islam 101," and was aired shortly after the September 11 events transpired. Another incredible role model was an Islamic man who appeared on a children's special hosted by Peter Jennings from ABC-News, aired the Saturday morning following the terrorist attacks. Both of these gentlemen raised *our* consciousness, so why not the consciousness of Islam?

THE CHOICE BETWEEN DARKNESS AND LIGHT

"We have not fallen into crisis after crisis because our ideals have failed but because we have never applied them. A return to the highest hopes and dreams of the Founding Fathers might rescue us. We determine which future we create by the views we hold."

— ROBERT THEOBALD
1929-1999

Deeply etched in my consciousness is a scene from the Gulf War — a profound example of compassion exhibited by American soldiers when they encoun-tered Iraqi soldiers who wished to surrender. Not wanting to be killed, the Iraqis pleaded for their lives and remarkably our soldiers did not shoot. Although you could see the fear and anxiety written on the faces of the Americans as they weighed the potentials before them — perhaps this 'surrender' was a trap they were being lulled into — they exercised restraint. They did not react in fear or vengeance; they saw other human beings and responded as a human being — with compassion. They chose the light. They passed the test.

> "Once to every man and nation comes the moment to decide…and the choice goes by forever 'twixt that darkness and that light."
> — JAMES RUSSELL LOWELL
> *1819-1891*

How will we know if our soulution meets the criteria of the next level of awareness? Here's the litmus test:

> "When in doubt, always err on the side of compassion. The test of whether you are helping or hurting: Are your fellow humans enlarged or reduced as a result of your help? Have you made them bigger or smaller? More able or less able?"
> — NEALE DONALD WALSCH
> *Conversations with God - Book 2 - pg 170*

How will we respond to this atrocity? Will we choose the path of least resistence, or rise to the next level of consciousness?

> "This is the moment of truth for humankind. Critical choices must now be made in order to protect the continued existence of human society and of the Earth itself."
> — ADI DA SAMRAJ
> *The Peace Law*

"We are the ones who have the most profound task in human history: the task of deciding whether we grow or die."

— JEAN HOUSTON

"Crisis in America," September 2001 www.jeanhouston.org

"This is a huge test we find ourselves in. We have newly emerged from a century of war and holocaust. Our hopes for the new century, the new millennium, were for a new way of being between nations and people, between earth and ourselves, between spirit and matter. These hopes still live, if anything, they have become more powerful, more necessary. For America it will mean a shift of our attitudes to other cultures around the world. To one of service and support rather than exploitation and dominance. Yes, the perpetrators have to be dealt with through therapeutic law and international justice. They are not a nation, they are a cancer, and a cancer is rarely removed through a cycle of violence. Rather...they have to be subdued by the strengthening of the immune system, the envisioning of the pattern of health, and yes, the removal of the cancer."

— JEAN HOUSTON

"Crisis in America," September 2001 www.jeanhouston.org

Let's now explore how you can contribute your incredible power to help heal our nation and the world.

CHAPTER XIV

Soulution Part II: Achieving Peace Through Authentic Power

"All oppression rises in our time. All shadows, all terrors, and factors unique in human history also arise around us to confound our folly and confuse our desire. We yearn for meaning and deal with trivia. We are swept in currents over which we have no control. Government has become too big for the small problems of life and too small in spirit for the large problems. The tyranny that threatens to destroy us is not just terrorism; it is the tyranny of the unjust demands we have made of nature and the tyranny of some nations being kept in economic slavery by other nations."

— JEAN HOUSTON
"Crisis in America," September 2001 www.jeanhouston.org

"Character comes from following our highest sense of right, from trusting ideals without being sure they'll work. One challenge of our adventure on Earth is to rise above dead systems — wars, religions, nations, destructions — to refuse to be a part of them, and express instead the highest selves we know how to be."

— RICHARD BACH
One - pg 114

"This tragedy brings us together in shadow and light, in richer and poorer, in sickness and in health for as long as we all shall live. The desecration that occurred is also the announcement of a potential global union... In light of the events of September 11th, we now must speak of the world heart, the world stomach, the world spirit. America is no longer insulated from the pathos of other nations."

— JEAN HOUSTON
"Crisis in America," September 2001 www.jeanhouston.org

Part II of our soulution utilizes our authentic power more fully. To begin, we would create a Vision Statement that defines what we want and articulates the highest vision of Who We Choose to Be. After defining our Vision, we will be able to function from a position of clarity and centeredness. Solutions to problems will become clear; maybe not comfortable, but clear. All decisions from that day forward will be made with conviction, free of doubt, and capable of rising above the powerful influences of self-interest — those whose motives are inconsistent with our highest vision: The betterment of humanity.

The Declaration of Independence was essentially our forefather's Vision Statement. And though the Civil War was fought under the guise of 'states rights,' the underlying catalyst was a breach in our country's Vision Statement. If our forefathers intended to *be* who they unequivocally stated they were, a nation who believed that "all men are created equal," they *had* to take action against slavery. Had they failed to act, they would have committed the highest breech of all: *The betrayal of Self.*

To more fully comprehend the need for an updated Vision Statement, a "Declaration of *Inter*dependence," I have utilized an underlying concept conveyed in *Gift from the Sea* by Anne Morrow Lindbergh and applied it to a Nation's Vision Statement:

Our Vision Statement does not simply articulate who we choose to be. It defines our purpose, what we believe in, and our responsibility to one another. Our Vision Statement articulates those objectives so specifically that there is no question as to how to remain centered and balanced when confronted with either an adversary or issue of great importance. It fully recognizes the existence of centrifugal opposing forces that will attempt to pull us from our center. However, our Vision Statement provides us the strength to remain strong and centered regardless of the shocks that come in at the periphery of our wheel that attempt to crack its hub.

Additionally, our Vision Statement would proclaim our conviction in helping to maintain the honor and dignity of every nation in our world, the sanctity of all life, and the beauty and necessity of diversity. It would proclaim the truth: That each person on this planet is interconnected and interdependent, that what we do to one another, we do to ourselves. Our Vision would convey our resolve for all human beings to be given the knowledge and opportunity from which to enjoy life, liberty, and the pursuit of happiness. After formulating our Vision Statement, we would then focus on what it *feels* like to live that Vision as if we already were. Then, we would simply allow the Law of Attraction 'do its thing' and await the appropriate people, events, and circumstances that will 'miraculously' actualize our Vision.

"THE EARTH CHARTER"

"We must join together to bring a sustainable global society founded on respect for nature, universal human rights, economic justice, and a culture of peace. Towards this end, it is imperative that we, the peoples of Earth, declare our responsibility to one another, to the greater community of life, and to future generations."
— FROM THE PREAMBLE OF THE EARTH CHARTER
www.earthcharter.org

Much to my amazement, I recently discovered that many people *have* been working on a Vision Statement for the world over the past ten years! In the aftermath of WWII, the world was ready and willing to do whatever was necessary to ensure peace.

People had seen enough bloodshed, lost enough sons, husbands, and fathers to seek solutions that did not include violence and death as options for settling disputes. From that desire, the United Nations was born. Its objective? To maintain world security and avert future wars by providing an open and public forum from which a country could air and settle its grievances with others. As the world evolved, however, it was clear that the United Nations charter was not expansive enough. So, in 1987, the United Nations World Commission on Environment and Development, as well as many other organizations and individuals around the world, called for "a new charter…to maintain our shared planet, and guide state behavior in the transition to sustainable development." As a result, work on the "Earth Charter," a declaration of interdependence and principles for sustainable development, began. Receiving input from thousands of people representing fifty-six countries, the final document was approved in March of 2000 and now awaits endorsement by the United Nations General Assembly in 2002.

The Earth Charter acknowledges that the fates of all humans are not only tied to one another, but to the larger environment of which we are all a part. It further states that humanity's environmental, economic, social, political, cultural, ethical, and spiritual problems and aspirations are interconnected, and that only *together* can we forge inclusive solutions. At the heart of the Earth Charter are four principles:

1. Respect the Earth and life in all its diversity

2. Care for the community of life with understanding, love, and compassion

3. Build democratic societies that are just, participatory, sustainable, and peaceful

4. Secure Earth's bounty and beauty for present and future generations

> *"As never before in history, common destiny beckons us to seek a new beginning. It requires a change of mind and heart. It requires a new sense of global interdependence and universal responsibility."*

At the conclusion of the Earth Charter it is stated:

> *"Let ours be a time remembered for the awakening of a new reverence for life, the firm resolve to achieve sustainability, the quickening of the struggle for justice and peace, and the joyful celebration of life."*

Let's take the Earth Charter even further and add to this wonderful vision the knowledge of our authentic power, so this vision becomes the probability we actualize. For if we 'push against' what we deem to be wrong in our world, we now know that we will only manifest *more* of what is wrong.

AUTHENTIC POWER?
THE POWER OF THOUGHT

Let's now explore the steps required to achieve peace utilizing our authentic power — the power of thought.

> *"You are not here to cry about the miseries of the human condition but to change them when you find them not to your liking through the joy, strength, and vitality that is within you."*
> — JANE ROBERTS
> *The Nature of Personal Reality - A Seth Book - pg 26*

Although you may be feeling powerless to effect any kind of change because our government's response to terrorism is well under way, you can indeed make a difference. Never underestimate your authentic power, for it can move mountains.

> *"Never doubt that a small group of thoughtful committed people can change the world, indeed it's the only thing that ever has."*
> — MARGARET MEAD
> *1901-1978*

How do we ensure a lasting peace? As John Lennon stated: *"All you need is love."* And though the thought of 'love' may seem fanciful, even ludicrous to some, Mr. Lennon was not speaking of sentimental 'kissy-kissy' love, he was referring to the highest, fastest, most pure frequency of energy.

"Man must evolve for all human conflict a method which rejects revenge, aggression, and retaliation. The foundation of such a method is love."

— MARTIN LUTHER KING JR
1929-1968

"If there is love, there is hope to have real families, real brotherhood, real equanimity, real peace. If the love within your heart is lost, if you continue to see others as enemies, then no matter how much knowledge or education you have, no matter how much material progress is made, only suffering and confusion will ensue. Human beings will continue to deceive and overpower one another... The foundation of all spiritual practice is love. That you practice well is my only request."

— THE DALI LAMA

PEACE ON EARTH
HUMANITY'S INNERMOST QUEST

"Peace is that for which the world most yearns."
— THE ESSENE GOSPEL OF PEACE - BOOK 4
The Teachings of the Elect - pg 29

"All hatred driven hence, the soul recovers radical innocence and learns at last that it is self-delighting, self-appeasing, self-affrighting, and that its own sweet will is Heaven's will."

— W. B. YEATS
1856-1939

"The problem with world peace is that the individual feels helpless, but the answer to that is not complicated. A man can do something for peace in our world without having to jump into politics. Each man has inside him a basic decency and goodness. If he listens to it and acts upon it, he is giving a great deal of what it is the world needs most. It is not complicated, but it takes courage. It takes courage for a man to listen to his own goodness and act upon it. Do we dare to be ourselves? That is the question that counts."

— PABLO CABALS
1876-1973

"Hatred of war will not bring peace.... Only love of peace will bring about those conditions."

— JANE ROBERTS
The Nature of Personal Reality - Seth Book - pg 32

When my son Zachary (now 11) was in the third grade, his class celebrated Dr. Martin Luther King Jr.'s birthday, and "I have a dream" vision for our world. The children cut out the form of a dove, the sign of peace, and articulated their dream on one side, and on the other, the parents articulated theirs. At a school open-house a few weeks later, the doves were prominently displayed in the classroom. As I read each of them I was amazed, for the majority of doves shared an identical dream: "To live in a peaceful world where all people loved one another despite their differences." Perhaps that objective is instinctive to humanity.

Peace on Earth can only be achieved by utilizing an approach we have never before considered. It requires the knowledge of an advanced form of thinking, a quantum leap of enormous magnitude into an unknown realm. This approach was articulated in *Emissary of Light* by author and musician James Twyman. After performing a peace concert in Bosnia-Croatia, an area riddled in hatred and war for centuries, Mr. Twyman was led to a secret group called "The Emissaries of Light" where he was given a message and asked to deliver it to the world:

> *"The world is now ready to begin adulthood and take responsibility for itself. Humanity has finally reached a stage of evolution where it understands the futility of war."*

When Mr. Twyman wanted to know specifically how a lasting peace could be achieved, he was told that it simply required a tiny shift in consciousness:

> *"When you came here, you thought the work we do was going to bring peace to the world. You perceived a violent world, then set up the circumstances that would make it peaceful. This isn't what the Emissaries do at all. We don't perceive a violent world. It's that simple. We see a world that is living with the illusion of violence, and we project the truth, an experience of peace...Lasting peace will never come to a world that thinks it has a choice between peace and war... 'Seek not peace here' means do not try to fix a world that was born from the idea of*

conflict. Look past that vision of the world. Seek peace where it really is, within you. Then extend that peace wherever you are, to whoever you meet. Then the world that was born from conflict will change by itself. It will begin to reflect the new choice you made, the choice to see peace where it really is...Do not believe those that tell you that you must change the world. It is easy to see that such attempts have always brought temporary results at best. Change your mind about the world. See the world as an extension of your mind. Find peace and love within and it will automatically project itself outward into the world... Peace is everywhere. You can choose to see peace, or you can choose to see violence... Stop trying to bring peace to war. Bring peace to peace and then you'll know what you're to do. Humanity is waiting for this message... The world has been waiting for people to tell the truth, the truth they have always felt inside them, but that they could never quite identify. But, most of all, teach what you have learned, that they are ready to take a new step, a step so tiny it will hardly be noticed. And yet this tiny step is a leap past the conflict and fear that has seemed so real for so long. Humanity is ready, but it must believe it is ready."

— JAMES TWYMAN
Emissary of Light - pp 200–203

It appears that the only obstacle to achieving peace on Earth lies in our perception, our belief, for our beliefs create our bias which, we now know, creates our reality. As we have learned, the circumstances of our lives simply indicate the frequencies we are currently attuned to. So by consciously tuning into different frequencies, in this case the frequency of peace, taking the tiniest of steps, we can actualize the probabilities we desire. What happens when we attune to a new frequency? As in our game of Nintendo,® now validated by the Emissaries, a sequence of events always follows a 'choice point.' In Physics, this sequence is referred to as the "Butterfly Effect" and is fundamental to the Chaos Theory. Author James Gleick in *Chaos: Making a New Science* defines the "Butterfly Effect" as: "The notion that a butterfly stirring the air today in Peking can transform storm systems next month in New York."

> *"A tiny change today brings us to a dramatically different tomorrow."*
> — RICHARD BACH
> *One - pg 143*

Are *you* willing to take that tiny step and call forth peace within your life? Are you willing to focus your powerful thoughts on peace so that we can actualize a peaceful future? The prophecies indicated that the time has come where we must.

> *"You must be the change you wish to see in the world."*
> — MAHATMA GANDHI
> *1869-1948*

> *"It is dawning on us that ours is a time of profound, long-term cultural change and not just a time of more improvements to the world as we have known it."*
> — RUBEN NELSON
> *Reflections on Paradigms - 1993*
> *a paper prepared for The Environment Council of Alberta, Canada*

CHAPTER XV

Soulution Part III: Self-Confrontation: Cleaning up Our Own Backyard

"The test of a civilized person [nation] is first self-awareness, and then depth after depth of sincerity in self-confrontation."

— CLARENCE DAY
1874-1935

"The psychological rule says that when an inner situation is not made conscious, it happens outside, as fate. That is to say, when the individual remains undivided and does not become conscious of his inner contradictions, the world must perforce act out the conflict and be torn into opposite halves."

— CARL JUNG
1875-1961

"Thank God, our time is now, when wrong comes up to meet us everywhere, never to leave us till we take the longest stride of soul men ever took."
— CHRISTOPHER FRY

"Our ability to block our experience is an evolutionary dead end. Rather than experiencing and transforming pain, conflict, and fear, we often divert or dampen them with a kind of unwitting hypnosis."
— MARILYN FERGUSON
The Aquarian Conspiracy - pg 75

"The world is in the condition it is in because of you, and the choices you have made — or failed to make. (Not to decide is to decide.) The Earth is in the shape it's in because of you, and the choices you have made — or failed to make. Your own life is the way it is because of you, and the choices you have made — or failed to make."
— NEALE DONALD WALSCH
Conversations with God - Book 1 - pg 50

"Denial, however human and natural a response, exacts a terrible price.... It doesn't work. A part of the self keenly feels all the denied pain."
— MARILYN FERGUSON
The Aquarian Conspiracy - pg 75

In *The Study of History,* English historian Arnold Toynbee (1889-1975) concluded that twenty-six civilizations perished because they had refused to evolve. They had become so rigid in their belief systems, so snug in their comfort zones, so dazzled by their power and brilliance, that they stagnated and failed to move into the next meme. The result? They unwittingly devised their own demise.

To avoid the fate of those civilizations, it is imperative that we meet the challenge before us. Part III of our soulution helps us to achieve this goal by cleaning up our own backyards. In terms of energy, this means to identify and transmute a negative attractor field to positive, for that negative energy has created an imbalance in our beings — an imbalance that is preventing us from moving forward in our evolution.

> *"Progressing to a more elevated condition is only possible when the backlog [of unlearned lessons] can be processed, providing us with new under-standing and insights of past mistakes as we go."*
> — MOIRA TIMMS
> *Beyond Prophecies and Predictions - pg 34*

To identify a negative attractor field, we must candidly look ourselves, as a nation, in the mirror. The issue of self-confrontation is most challenging for it is difficult to acknowledge our 'shadow self,' especially when we have only thought of ourselves as a generous and compassionate nation. However, the stakes are now high. If humankind is to remain on this planet, we must muster the courage to address some uncomfortable issues before they explode in our faces and all of us are gone.

Let's begin with a basis of understanding: Those of us in America form an entity composed of our collective energies. The choices we made or failed to make produced 'evidence' — people, events, or circumstances, that corresponded with what we chose or neglected. Typically, the underlying cause of 'stuck' energy is one of two things: repressed issues from our past, or a belief we are holding that opposes what we want, thereby creating a conflict, or imbalance, in energy.

Because we must first identify what we don't want *before* we can use our power to magnetize what we want, we must uncover the decisions we made or failed to make that helped to create the explosion of energy we experienced on September 11. What grievances do others have with us? If others allege that we exploit them — that we rape and pillage their land and then leave, we need to take a hard look in the mirror and honestly ask ourselves if we do. We must determine how we responded in the past when confronted with a perceived injustice by others. Did we assume the role of patriarch, one where we listened, empathized, and searched for a solution, or did we respond as the big powerful United States who didn't have the time nor patience to listen to the petty grievances of those who didn't directly impact our lives? Each of our responses created energy — good or bad — that added to a vortex of energy that exploded on September 11.

Shortly after September 11, I received another email that explained why some in the MidEast had become disgruntled with America. While on an editorial assignment a few years ago, Gotham Chopra, son of the acclaimed author Deepak Chopra, received a first-hand look at Islamic military training based in Pakistani religious schools. In these infamous schools, young Muslim boys are 'programmed' into hostile anti-western terrorists. When introduced to the chancellor of one of these schools, Gotham was greeted warmly. He began his interview asking why the United States was so hated, and the chancellor eloquently recounted the history of the U.S. and Afghanistan as allies in the cold war against the Soviet regime. But as the chancellor moved deeper into this history, his tone began to expose the deep hostility and animosity he felt for America:

> "You gave us weapons and trained our men. You built our roads, fed our people. You made us your friend. But then your cold war ended and you deserted us. Because it was no longer in your selfish interest to have us as your allies, you abandoned us — left our people hungry and hateful. You turned your friends into foes because you treated us like whores."

He then looked at Chopra and stated:

> "Today you are our guest. If we were not hospitable, we would be very ashamed. But in times of war, yes, you would be an enemy and we may kill you. Today a friend, tomorrow, inshallah (God willing), there will not be one."

Clearly we can see the evolution and growth of hatred. The energy of a perceived injustice, however true or distorted it may or may not be, begins to magnetize more of the same energy until it grows large enough to commit mass murder. Therefore, it is imperative that we prevent those seeds from being sown — to address the needs of our friends around the globe, admit the wrongs of our past, and ask forgiveness for our past errors. That is, if we *really* want peace.

"WALKING THE TALK"

A shining example of 'walking the talk' and paving the way for others to follow is seen in the recent actions of Pope John Paul II, the most influential religious leader in our world. In a number of unprecedented moves, he is *doing* exactly what we are speaking of here — cleaning up the backyard of the Catholic Church.

Pope John Paul II is going where no Pope has gone before, for he feels that without acknowledging the wrongs of the past and wiping the slate clean, peace will never come to our world. Furthermore, he feels that the church would be incapable of fulfilling its Mission of providing a guiding light of hope, love, and faith for people if the past is not healed, for under those circumstances, it could only be seen as hypo-critical.

Bestowed with the honor of Time Magazine's 1994 "Man of the Year," John Paul has demonstrated great humility. Despite his ailing health and frailty, he has traveled to areas that had schisms with the Catholic Church asking pardon for his church's acts of sins, omissions, and numerous errors made in the past two thousand years.

In March of 2000, he did something even more startling when he released a document entitled *"Memory and Reconciliation: The Church and its Past Errors."* In this breakthrough document, the Pope acknowledges the church's involvement and guilt for its inaction in the Jewish holocaust, its participation in the Spanish Inquisition, its persecution of Galileo for his scientific discoveries that defied the church's beliefs, its involvement in the Crusades, as well as its participation in the downfall of Constantinople which led to a rift with the Orthodox church. Going even further, John Paul has taken extraordinary steps to seek unity with all major faiths, visiting both a mosque and synagogue.

As you may have surmised, not all Catholics embrace the Pope's bold gestures, for many feel that the church can do no wrong. Those who oppose his actions feel that the Pope is humiliating the church, distorting its past, and paying respect to its persecutors. A man of great vision and conviction though, he is listening to both his heart and to the "Big Guy," and for that, I am profoundly grateful. In my estimation, he is the "Man of the Millennium," and by the way, I am not Catholic.

"Expanding one's consciousness [like increasing the light in a dark room] and raising one's vibration are synonymous...Dealing with one's inner issues, past traumas, and old habit patterns are part of what it takes to unload the ballast of the past, and prepares one to receive more light and function at a higher vibratory rate [frequency of energy]."

— MOIRA TIMMS
Beyond Prophecies and Predictions - pg 11

In order to evolve, we must now have the courage to follow in Pope John Paul's footsteps and acknowledge and heal *our* previous errors, omissions, and "sins."

"'Love one another.' This gentle precept, which two thousand years ago came like a soothing oil humbly poured on human suffering, offers itself to our modern spirit as the most powerful, and in fact the only imaginable, principle of the earth's future equilibrium. Shall we at last make up our minds to admit that it is neither weakness nor harmless fad — but that it points out a formal condition for the achievement of life's most organic and most technically advanced progress? If we did so decide, what awaits us would be the true victory and the only true peace. In its own heart, force would be constrained to disarm, because we should at last have laid our hands on a stronger weapon with which to replace it. And man, grown to his full stature, would have found the right road."

— PIERRE TEILHARD DE CHARDIN
1881-1955 Activation of Energy - pg 20

CHAPTER XVI

Soulution Part IV:
Living at the Next Level of Consciousness

"In my dream, the Angel shrugged and said 'If we fail this time, it will be a failure of imagination.' And then she placed the world gently in the palm of my hand."

— BRIAN ANDREAS
Still Mostly True

"Instead of looking at life through a rear-view mirror, look before you and behold the current possibilities with innocent perception... Forgive yourself and others, for yesterday has already been lived... Be here now and face the path in front of you, for that is where life is."

— GLENDA GREEN
Love Without End: Jesus Speaks - pg 169

"What you have done is unimportant compared to what you are about to do. How you have erred is insignificant compared to how you are about to create."

— NEALE DONALD WALSCH
Conversations with God - Book 3 - pg 87

"All power is given man to bring his Heaven upon his Earth, and this is the goal of the 'Game of Life.' The simple rules are fearless faith, nonresistance, and love!"

— FLORENCE SHOVEL SHINN
The Writings of Florence Shovel Shinn 'The Game' - pg 89

"A human being is part of a whole, called by us the 'Universe,' a part limited in time and space. He experiences himself, his thoughts and his feelings, as something separated from the rest — a kind of optical delusion of his consciousness. This delusion is a kind of prison for us, restricting us to our personal desires and to affection for a few persons nearest us. Our task must be to free ourselves from this prison by widening our circles of compassion to embrace all living creatures and the whole of nature in its beauty."

— ALBERT EINSTEIN
1879-1955

The time has come to live consciously, to utilize the latent powers within each and every one of us to create lives filled with joy and magic. The knowledge and tools needed to create our future realities have now been revealed, allowing us to integrate all aspects of our body/mind/spirit, and live in joy, harmony, peace, love, kindness, compassion, and gratitude. This does not mean that all negative will be abolished in our world, for the negative is required to foster evolution. It means that each of us, as individuals, will now be able to choose whether to participate in the creations of others or not.

MAKING THE SHIFT INTO THE NEXT LEVEL OF CONSCIOUSNESS

"The mighty labor now being generated to wrest new life from the clutches of the old will not be easy. In human affairs, age tends to crystallize one's ideas; and, in the same sense, our culture is now cracking under the weight of its own senile tenacity to status quo. The task at hand is to release that which no longer serves us and retain the best from all that we have accomplished to serve as a platform upon which the 'New Order of the Ages' will be secured."

— MOIRA TIMMS
Beyond Prophecies and Predictions - pg 48

Regardless of the meme each of us now calls 'home sweet home,' the "Shift of Ages" stipulates that each of us must transition into the next higher meme. This will be challenging, for this transformation is not only a paradigm shift of enormous magnitude, but is made even more intense with the increase of the Schumann Resonance —— the acceleration of energy now occurring in our world. This increase in energy can be thought of as *"Pitocin®,"* a drug given to women to induce labor, thus hastening the birth of a new child — however reluctant he or she might be to leave the womb (comfort zone).

We are now in the throes of labor — big-time. Humanity is on the threshold of giving birth to a new stage of consciousness. You, as an individual, are being given the rare opportunity to take a giant step in your evolution; a step that could be likened to a move in the game of *"Sorry":®* When you have the good fortune of landing on a specific square, you are able to "slide" forward, or bypass, five squares, allowing you to reach your destination more rapidly.

In spite of the forthcoming positive changes, powerful whirlwinds of negative energy are now pervading our world. Therefore, it has never been more important to begin utilizing your authentic power. This may initially feel awkward, as though you are being required to use your left hand when you're right-handed. But just as you fell off of your bicycle a number of times before you learned to ride effortlessly, the same is true of living in authentic power. Initially, it will require practice to find your balance.

> *"No man gives to himself but himself, and no man takes away from himself but himself: the 'Game of Life' is a game of solitaire; as you change, all conditions will change."*
> — FLORENCE SHOVEL SHINN
> The Writings of Florence Shovel Shinn "The Secret Door" - pg 197

THE GIFT OF A FEELING FREQUENCY

To assist in our transformation, we were given a precious gift immediately following the September 11 tragedies: The gift of a feeling frequency — what it *feels* like to live consciously as a human family. After experiencing the unprecedented outpouring of love, compassion, and kindness, as well as observing people transcend their fundamental beliefs that typically would have repelled one from another, a new frequency was made available to us — one we can access at any time.

How do we utilize this frequency? Whenever you encounter adverse feelings, people, events, or circumstances, simply close your eyes and 'remember' those uplifting experiences. Focus on how you felt as you witnessed those scenes of love, kindness, and compassion. Then, through the Law of Attraction, you will begin to magnetize experiences imbued with that same feeling frequency into your life. And as you do, you will begin to recognize just how powerful you really are.

If you need more information to ease your transition into the next meme, I will shamelessly plug my book *Life: A Complete Operating Manual,* for *"Life"* is a workbook and guide designed to lead you step-by-step through all we have discussed and much more. After answering a series of questions, you will be able to identify your "stuck ch'i," learn how to jettison it from your energy field, and then rebuild your comfort zone to something that resembles a beautiful mansion rather than a shanty with a leaky roof. It's work, but it's well worth it to begin living consciously.

The time has come for the seat of power, now held by science, to pass onto the next meme. What are the attributes of this new meme? This stage of development integrates all the preceding memes, recognizing each for its contribution to the whole. It is a meme characterized by a decrease in narcissism, an increase in compassion, and the ability to see the 'bigger picture.' At this meme, dialogue and relationship-building is emphasized, for as we progress higher and higher through the various memes, we grow in wisdom and experience, allowing for a more holistic integral approach to life. Sound good?

WILL YOU LEND A HELPING HAND?

"What do we live for, if it is not to make life less difficult for each other?"
— GEORGE ELIOT
(Mary Ann Evans) 1819-1880

"Give a man a fish, and you feed him for a day. Teach a man to fish, and you feed him for a lifetime."
— CHINESE PROVERB

"Anticipate charity by preventing poverty; assist the reduced fellow man, either by a considerable gift, or a sum of money, or by teaching him a trade, or putting him in the way of business, so that he may earn an honest livelihood, and not be forced to the dreadful alternative of holding out his hand for charity. This is the highest step and the summit of charity's golden ladder."

— MAIMONDES
1135-1204

The greatest gift you can give to another is the gift of themselves: the gift of their authentic power. However, keep in mind that people are not generally open to new information, especially that which is life-changing, unless they are experiencing some form of discomfort in their lives. This may put you in an awkward position, for now that you have a more expansive awareness of the 'bigger picture,' you will be able to see issues and their solutions more clearly, and some folks may not be interested in your newly-discovered knowledge. In those instances, bite your tongue and recognize that each of us is a sacred soul on a sacred journey and must find his or her own truth. And bear in mind that all paths lead to the same destination.

"The right of choice is your freedom. You can stay lost as long as you want, and you can come home when you're ready. In the meantime, you may experience all the lessons that the denial of love can bring you!"

— GLENDA GREEN
Love Without End: Jesus Speaks - pg 147

Today, however, not only are many people open, but hungering for this information. They may have received personal 'wake-up' calls through job layoffs, the declining stock market, a crippled economy, etc. Just keep in mind the following two concepts if you choose to share this revolutionary information: "Fight or flee," and "Ask and it is given." If someone is genuinely interested in what you have to say they will *ask* for more information. On the other hand, if they're not interested they will either "flee," or you may become the target of a "fight."

"From the sleep of a million starless dreams, the pulse of the planet quickens. Restless, and deep within its being, a vision from the mists of consciousness awakes. Through myth and symbol, an externalizing force uncoils as yawning synapses gently spark silent predawn currents of a new birth. In this perfect waking moment, all life listens, holds its breath, changing focus as the void of darkness yields its shadows to the young light. The presence of the new day is all around....permeating, invisible, throughout and within. The labor has begun...new life awaits. Take a deep breath...."

— MOIRA TIMMS
Beyond Prophecies and Predictions - pg 303

CHAPTER XVII

Humankind at a Crossroads

"Someday, after we have mastered the winds, the waves, the tide, and gravity, we shall harness for God the energies of love. Then, for the second time in the history of the world, we will have discovered fire."

— PIERRE TEILHARD DE CHARDIN
1881-1955

"We stand on the brink of a new age, the age of an open world, a time of renewal when a fresh release of spiritual energy in the world culture may unleash new possibilities. The sum of our days is just beginning."

— LEWIS MUMFORD
1895-1990

"Whispers of change are stealing over the face of the world once more. Like another vast dream beginning, man's consciousness is slowly spreading outwards once again. Some voice from the long ago is divinely trumpeting across our little globe."

— EDMOND BORDEAUX SZEKELEY
The Gospel of the Essenes - pg 124

"For by involution and evolution shall the salvation of all the world be accomplished: by the Descent of Spirit into matter, and the Ascent of matter into Spirit through the ages."

— THE GOSPEL OF THE HOLY TWELVE
The Essene New Testament - pg 149

In Stanley Kubrick's legendary movie depiction of *"2001: A Space Odyssey,"* written by Arthur Clarke, a black monolith mysteriously emerges each time humankind is ready to evolve into the next level of consciousness. I believe the September 11 tragedies represent that monolith and that we are being called upon to evolve *now.*

"Come, my friends. 'Tis not too late to seek a newer world."

— ALFRED LORD TENNYSON
1809-1892

It has taken generations and generations of those who came before us to build the bridges and create the potential for the rebirth of our world. Now it's up to us to *actualize* this dream — the probability of "Heaven on Earth." We have been given the keys to the kingdom. Will we heed this opportunity? Will we have the wisdom to respond to the events of September 11 at the next level of awareness? Will we have the courage to clean our backyard? Will you BE who you really are?

"To be or not to be: That is the question."
— WILLIAM SHAKESPEARE
1564-1616

At the close of *Indigo Children,* a best-selling book that sheds a new light on the recent 'epidemic' of ADD in children *(attention deficit disorder)* by coauthors Lee Carroll and Jan Tober, an interesting excerpt is included that was written by an unknown author. And though I acknowledge that I am taking the risk of pushing you 'over the edge,' this passage speaks volumes about this precise moment in history. I only hope that it helps to confirm in your heart that the events of September 11 indeed had a higher purpose: that the three thousand forty-four cherished souls who perished on that fateful day catalyzed the dawning of the most magnificent era that humankind has ever experienced. But once more, that is my belief and you must find your own.

"The time of the Great Awakening is come. You who have chosen to lift your eyes from darkness to the light are blessed to see the event of a new day on planet Earth. Because your heart has yearned to see real peace where war has reigned, to show mercy where cruelty has dominated, and to know love where fear has frozen hearts, you are privileged to your world.

Planet Earth is a blessing to you. She is your friend and your Mother. Always remember and honor your relationship with her. She is a living, loving, breathing being, like unto yourself. She feels the love that you give as you walk upon her soil with a happy heart.

The Creator has chosen your hands to reach the lonely, your eyes to see innocence, not guilt, and your lips to utter words of comfort. Let pain be no more! You have wandered in dark dreams for so long now. Step into the light and send for what you know is truth. The world has suffered, not from evil, but from fear of acknowledgment of the good. Allow fear to be released now and forever — released into the light and transformed. It is within your power to do so.

No one can find yourself but you. All your answers are within. Teach the lessons you have learned. Your understanding has been given, not only for yourself, but to guide a sore and tired world to a place of rest in a new consciousness. Here before you is your vision come true. Here is your answer given you — a song to soothe a weary soul and make it new again. Here is the bridge that joins you to your brothers and sisters. Here is your Self. Look gently upon yourself and allow yourself to be filled by the Light you have been seeing.

True love comes from yourself, and every thought is a blessing to the entire Universe. All areas of your life will be healed. You will shine with a golden splendor that speaks of the One who created you in wisdom and glory. The past will dissolve like a dark dream, and your joy will be so brilliant that you will have no recollection of the night.

Go forth and be a messenger of Hope. Point the way to

healing by walking in gratefulness. Your brothers and sisters will follow. And as you pass beyond the portal of limitation, you will be united and reunited with all who seem to be lost. There is no loss in the Creator. Choose the path of forgiveness, and you will weep tears of joy for the goodness you find in all.

Go forth and live the life of the radiant soul that you are. Glorify the Creator in your every deed. You are important, you are needed, and you are worthy. Do not allow the dark cloak of fear to hide the light from your view. You were not born to fail. You were destined to succeed. The hope of the world has been planted in your breast, and you are assured of success as you stand for the One who created you. This, then, is the healing of Planet Earth. All your doubts and fears can be set aside, as you know the healing comes from the love in your heart." *pp 219–222*

In 1985, I received a very strange message, one I was unable to comprehend for more than ten years. You may find it interesting in light of the information presented in this book:

"Things only happen when you make them happen. To let go and surrender is to let things happen to you. You have free will and must set things in motion. Planet Earth is on the verge of destructive power in the wrong hands. Things will only change when people change. To raise people's spiritual consciousness is the task at hand. It can only begin there and be demonstrated as such. There is much work to do. Begin by helping others become aware. You have the gift. Use it or it will be wasted. This is your

Mission. D.M.A. [Dimensional Mind Approach — a course I was then taking at a local college that dealt with the multi-dimensions of the mind] is your first step. Everyone's 'universal truth' they espouse is holy unto them. Formulate your own truth, live by it, share it, and teach it. That is your Mission. To blend the psychological awareness of your past with the awareness of the reality of the future is the key. While men are building new and beautiful skyscrapers, energy should be channeled into consciousness into this world. They are blind — make them see. Various civilizations that were highly technical, fell. When there is technology without the awareness of God, it cannot work. God is before technology, and channeling the power properly will benefit and evolve mankind. It is time — the time is now for these events to happen. They only happen with individual people. That is the task at hand."

The cocoon is breaking open, the butterfly emerging. Beautiful days are before us for man is learning to fly!

It is my innermost wish that this message has filled your heart with hope, inspiration, and excitement for the days ahead. May your path be blessed with love, joy, and miracles.

From my heart to yours,

Lauren Tratar

Permissions

In honor, gratitude, and respect, I wish to acknowledge the following authors and publishers who have graciously granted permission to reprint passages from their copyrighted works:

INFINITE MIND: SCIENCE OF THE HUMAN VIBRATIONS OF CONSCIOUSNESS by Dr. Valerie Hunt © 1989, 1995, 1996 ISBN: 0-964 3988-1-8 Reprinted with permission from Malibu Publishing P.O. Box 4234 Malibu, CA 90265

BEYOND PROPHECIES AND PREDICTIONS: EVERYONE'S GUIDE TO THE COMING CHANGES by Moira Timms © 1980, 1994, 1996 ISBN: 0-345-41020-3 Reprinted with the permission of Moira Timms thinkvideo.com 1-800-493-3005

[Reuse of] passages totaling 185 words, from ONE by Richard Bach © 1988 by ALTERNATE FUTURES, INC. Reprinted by permission of HarperCollins Publishers Inc. 10 E. 53rd St., NY, NY 10022

Bibliography

The Bible Code by Michael Drosnin © 1997 ISBN: 108684284973-9 Touchstone Rockefeller Center 1230 Avenue of the America NY, NY 10020

The Gospel of the Essenes: The Unknown Books of the Essenes and Lost Scrolls of the Essene Brotherhood The original Hebrew and Aramaic texts translated and edited by Edmond Bordeaux Szekeley © 1974, 1976, 1998 ISBN: 0-85207-135-3C. W. Daniel Co., Ltd 1 Church Path, Saffron Walden, Essex, CB10 1JP England

The Discovery of the Essene Gospel of Peace: The Essenes and the Vatican by Edmond Bordeaux Szekeley © 1989 ISBN: 0-85964004X International Biogenic Society P.O. Box 849, Nelson, British Columbia, Canada V1L 6A5

The Essene Gospel of Peace Book 4: The Teachings of the Elect The original Hebrew and Aramaic texts translated and edited by Edmond Bordeaux Szekeley © 1981 ISBN: 0-895640031 International Biogenic Society P.O. Box 849 Nelson, British Columbia, Canada V1L 6A5

The Gospel of the Holy Twelve: The Essene New Testament translated from the original Aramaic by Reverend Gideon Jasper Ouseley (late 1800's) Published by: The Essene Church of Christ 45 N. 3rd Street, Creswell, Oregon 97426 www.essene.org

The Emerald Tablets of Thoth The-Atlantean translation and interpretation by Doreal ISBN: 0-9665312-0-5 Source Books P.O. Box 292231, Nashville, Tenn. 37229-2231

A Fourth Course of Chicken Soup for the Soul by Jack Canfield, Mark Victor Hansen, Hanoch McCarty and Melanee McCarty ©1997 ISBN: 1-55874-467-3 Health Communications Inc. 3201 SW 15th Street, Deerfield Beach, FL 33442-8190

Paradigms: The Business of Discovering the Future by Joel Arthur Barker ©1992 ISBN: 0-88730-647-0 Harper Business/ A Division of Harper Collins Publishers 10 E. 53rd Street, NY, NY 10022

Awakening to Zero Point: The Collective Initiation by Gregg Braden ©1997 ISBN: 1-889071-09-9 Radio Bookstore Press P.O. Box 3010, Bellevue, WA 98009-3010

A Course in Miracles® c/o The Founda-tion for Inner Peace ©1996 ISBN: 0-670-86975-9 Penguin Books USA Inc. 375 Hudson Street, NY, NY 10014

Gift From the Sea by Anne Morrow Lindbergh ©1983 ISBN: 0-679-73241-1 Published by Vintage Books/Random House Inc. 201 E. 50th Street, NY, NY 10022

Walking Between the Worlds: The Science of Compassion by Gregg Braden ©1997 ISBN: 1-889071-05-6 Radio Bookstore Press P.O. Box 3010 Bellevue, WA 98009

The Isaiah Effect: Decoding the Lost Science of Prayer and Prophecy by Gregg Braden ©2000 ISBN: 0-609-60534-8 Harmony Books 201 E. 50th Street, NY, NY 10022

Many Lives, Many Masters by Brian L. Weiss, M.D. ©1988 ISBN: 0-671-63786-0 A Fireside Book Published by Simon & Schuster, Inc.1230 Avenue of the Americas, NY, NY 10020

The Indigo Children by Lee Carroll and Jan Tober © 1999 by Lee Carroll and Jan Tober Published by Hay House, Inc. P.O. Box 5100, Carlsbad, CA 92018

A Theory of Everything by Ken Wilber © 2000 ISBN: 1-57062-724-X Shambhala Publications, Inc. Horticultural Hall 300 Massa-chusetts Avenue, Boston, MA

The Messengers by Julia Ingram and G.W. Hardin ©1996 ISBN: 0-671-01686-5 Pocket Books a division of Simon and Schuster 1230 Avenue of the Americas New York, NY

Anatomy of an Illness by Norman Cousins ©1979 ISBN: 0-553-01293-2 A Bantam Book/Published by arrangement with W.W. Norton & Co., Inc. 500 5th Avenue, New York, NY 10036

Anatomy of the Spirit by Carolyn Myss, Ph. D. ©1996 ISBN: 0-517-70391-2 Crown Publishers, Inc. 201 E. 50th New York, NY 10022

The Writings of Florence Scovel Shinn by Florence Scovel Shinn ©1988 ISBN: 0-87516-6105 DeVorss and Co. Publications P.O. Box 550 Marina Del Rey, CA 90294

A Course in Miracles® c/o The Foundation for Inner Peace ©1996 ISBN: 0-670-86975-9 Penguin Books USA Inc. 375 Hudson Street, New York, NY 10014

The Children of the Law of One and The Lost Teachings of Atlantis by Jon Peniel © 1997 ISBN: 0-9660015-0-8 www.atlantis.to

Creative Visualization by Shakti Gawain © 1978 ISBN: 0-553-24147-8 Whatever Publishing P.O. Box 137 Mill Valley, CA 94941

The HeartMath® *Solution: The Institute of HeartMath's Revolutionary Program for Engaging the Power of the Heart's Intelligence* by Doc Childre and Howard Martin © 1999 ISBN: 0-06-251065-1

To order your copy of

life

a complete operating manual

please call

1-888-762-7808

or visit our website at

www.secrettolife.NET

"I invite you to the Great Adventure. And on this adventure you are not to repeat spiritually what others have done before us, because our adventure begins from beyond that stage. We are now for a new creation, entirely new, carrying in it all the unforseen, all risks, all hazards — a true adventure... of which the way is unknown and has to be traced out step by step in the unexplored. It is something that has never been in the present universe and will never be in the same manner. If that interests you, well, 'embark'."

— MIRRA ALFASSA
1878-1973
known as "The Mother" who served with Sri Aurobindo in India